OLD TESTAMENT

Gordon McConville

TEACH YOURSELF BOOKS

Long-renowned as the authoritative source for self-guided learning – with more than 30 million copies sold worldwide – the *Teach Yourself* series includes over 200 titles in the fields of languages, crafts, hobbies, sports, and other leisure activities.

Library of Congress Catalog Card Number: on file.

First published in UK 1996 by Hodder Headline Plc, 338 Euston Road, London NW1 3BH

A catalogue record for this title is available from the British Library.

First published in US 1996 by NTC Publishing Group, 4255 West Touhy Avenue, Lincolnwood (Chicago), Illinois 60646 – 19975 U.S.A.

Typeset by Transet Limited, Coventry, England.
Printed in Great Britain by Cox & Wyman Ltd, Reading, Berkshire.

Impression number   10 9 8 7 6 5 4 3 2 1
Year   1999 1998 1997 1996

CONTENTS

Abbreviations

Biblical books:

Chr	Chronicles	Lam	Lamentations
Dan	Daniel	Lev	Leviticus
Deut	Deuteronomy	Mic	Micah
Eccl	Ecclesiastes	Neh	Nehemiah
Exod	Exodus	Num	Numbers
Ezek	Ezekiel	Prov	Proverbs
Gen	Genesis	Ps	Psalms
Hos	Hosea	Sam	Samuel
Isa	Isaiah	Song	Song of Songs
Jdg	Judges		
Jer	Jeremiah	And from the New Testament:	
Josh	Joshua	Eph	Ephesians
Kgs	Kings	Rev	Revelation

Texts:

ANET	Ancient Near Eastern Texts
LXX	Septuagint translation of the Old Testament
MT	Masoretic Text

BCE	Before Common Era
CE	Common Era

INTRODUCTION

—————— **The Old Testament as** ——————
Scripture of Three Faiths

A volume on the Old Testament finds a natural place in a series on
World Faiths. This is not because it is the scripture of one faith in
particular (unlike the New Testament or the Qur'an). For the Old
Testament is scripture to Christianity, Judaism and Islam. This makes
it unique among the holy books. And the fact that it is shared is perhaps
one of the most important things about it. The modern world, for all its
secularism, is still shaped to a large extent by religion, a fact that
surfaces all too often in conflict. Meeting-points, therefore, are
extremely important. And the Old Testament can claim to be one of
these.

And yet, as the scripture of three religions, it might be said that the
Old Testament is three different things at once. For Christianity, it
contains the promises of Jesus Christ, the Messiah, the saviour of all
humanity. For Judaism, it is the Torah, given by God to Moses on
Mount Sinai, and authoritative rule of life. For Islam, it is the story of
the founders of the faith, Abraham and Ishmael, and of the prophets
who were forerunners to Muhammad.

Perhaps, then, the Old Testament is more a dividing-point than a
meeting-point! While each religion claims it, it does so on its own
terms. For none of them does it stand alone as scripture. The very
name the 'Old Testament' is at home, strictly, in Christianity, which
has a *New* Testament. This does not mean that in Christianity the Old

has no further function. But it does mean that it is interpreted through the eyes of the New. And the same thing happens in the other religions. Jews read the Old Testament (or Hebrew Bible, as they would prefer to call it, for obvious reasons) through their later scriptures, the Mishnah and Talmud. And Muslims do so via the Qur'an.

The reality of this 'sharing', then, is that there might be no common ground at all, or even a shunning of it. And this scarcely needs illustration, when the Old Testament plays a role in the politics of the Middle East. On one side, a direct appeal to it is the basis of a claim to land. On the other, that claim is totally rejected, and becomes a cause of deep resentment.

Yet there should be no counsel of despair. In Islam, the adherents of the three religions are known as 'the peoples of the Book'. And although they have received it differently, there is still a place for sharing its study. Followers of each of the religions do well, in the first place, to explore their own scriptures carefully. And to do so in awareness of each other is not only informative, but helps to understand the processes of interpretation: why we are as we are, where we differ, and where we do not.

—— The Old Testament as Cultural —— Heritage

A second reason for studying the Old Testament is its contribution to the dominant culture in the western world. Like the Classics of ancient Greece and Rome, its literature has become part of our corporate memory. The names of Noah, Abraham, Joseph, Moses, Samson, Rahab, Ruth, David, Solomon, Jezebel, Daniel, Esther are a roll-call of characters who have passed into the common consciousness. In part this is due to medieval art and drama, which gave us Michelangelo's David, and countless other retellings of the Biblical history in glass and stone. These days, it is true, knowledge of the Bible is less to the forefront of people's minds. Joseph - the son of Jacob, who was sold into slavery by his jealous brothers, and rose in spite of them to be vizier of Egypt - is probably best known through the show *Joseph and his Amazing Technicolor Dreamcoat* ! And David may owe more to the novelist Joseph Heller than to Michelangelo.

The cultural legacy of the Old Testament goes deeper, however. It has helped us think about the meaning of existence in our world. The name of the Book of Genesis is still familiar, even if in the popular mind the advances of science seem to have made its account of human beginnings obsolete. The truth on that particular matter is more complex, as we shall see. But in any case, the memory of Genesis has the effect of posing again and again the possibility that the world had its origin in a creative act of God.

I believe, furthermore, that the Old Testament has had an effect on how we think, in ways that we are scarcely aware of. For example, it does not only raise the question about *whether* God created. It has had much to do with what we think of when we think of God at all. The idea of one God, a personal deity to whom people can relate, is not common to all religions, but has been firmly planted in the western consciousness by the Old Testament. So too has the idea of a created order, a world made for human enjoyment, accessible to people and for their good. And our understanding of the organization of human society has developed out of a biblical tradition.

These claims need to be backed up, and I will try to say why I think they can be made. In general, the Old Testament is more than the possession of the three monotheistic religions, but part of a broad cultural heritage. In that context, as well as in Christian theology, it is known as the 'Old Testament'. And that may be the best reason for referring to it generally as such in a book like this one.

——————— The Aim of this Book ———————

Our aim in what follows is to open the Old Testament to all who are interested. It is a study with many dimensions. It requires some understanding of the ancient world in which it came into existence, for it is not isolated from the political and social currents of that world. Closely related is the history of the period, amounting to at least a millennium, and perhaps much more. These two topics will occupy the first two chapters. We shall then be in a position to consider the contents of the Old Testament systematically, together with the way in which the thirty-nine books were written. This is the largest part of the volume, and will take up the two middle chapters. Two final chapters then turn to interpretation, and the sorts of questions with which we began this introduction. How *do* Christians and Jews in particular make sense of the Old Testament, in relation to theological views that they hold? Furthermore, there are quite different, new ways of reading the Old Testament, that have opened up new possibilities for seeing its relevance to the modern world. As we shall see, Genesis has made a comeback in some surprising ways!

The Old Testament, finally, can hardly be read just for interest. It confronts the reader with God. And like it or not, he or she will be faced with some rather fundamental decisions.

1

THE OLD TESTAMENT
IN ITS WORLD

——— Israel in its Environment ———

The Birth of Civilization: Mesopotamia and Egypt

The first human civilizations flourished in some of the world's great river valleys: in the valleys of China's Yangtse and Yellow Rivers; in the Indus valley, to the north-west of the Indian sub-continent; in Mesopotamia, the 'land between the rivers', namely the Tigris and Euphrates; and in Egypt, along the great Nile. The latter two regions form the world of the Bible, at least for the greater part of the Old Testament period. Distinct from each other in terms of their development, their destinies were nevertheless linked because of geography. The journey from Mesopotamia to Egypt makes a great arc, often known as the 'fertile crescent', to distinguish it from the great dry zone of Arabia which lies to the south and east. The 'fertile crescent' stretches from the Persian Gulf to the Mediterranean and into Egypt. Around this arc flowed commerce and ideas, as well as political tensions and rivalries. The distinction between fertile and arid is one of the key factors, of course, in the rise of civilization itself. And it conditions the lives and thinking of the earliest humans, which have left us such a rich legacy not only in the Bible but in much other literature.

The earliest civilization in the region was the Sumerian, which was established by the end of the fourth millennium BCE. The origins of

THE ANCIENT NEAR EAST IN THE TIME OF THE PATRIARCHS

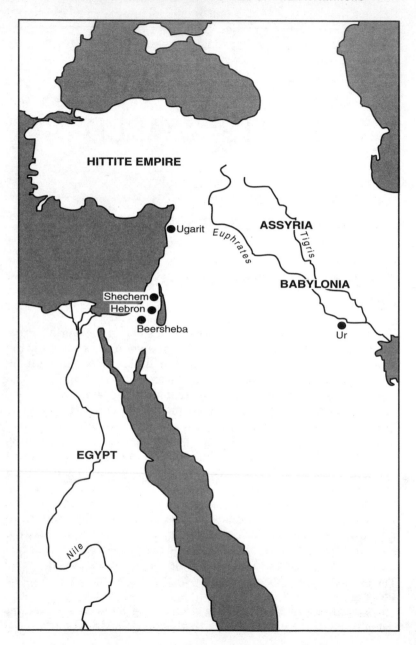

this people are unknown, but they dominated the region for more than a millennium. Already in the fourth millennium, they had developed the first culture based on cities, Uruk and Ur being among the most important. They invented writing, around 3200 BCE, perhaps for business purposes, but by the mid-second millennium they applied it to producing the first works of literature. Their legacy in this realm includes a flood-narrative, about which we shall hear more because of its relationship with the biblical narrative. Sumerians also made advances in astronomy, mathematics and architecture, government, art and craftsmanship, which have left their mark on modern civilization (for example the decimal system, and the division of time into hours and minutes). And they embarked on maritime trade, Ur being an important link between the Euphrates and the Persian Gulf.

The Sumerians were overrun at the beginning of the second millennium BCE by a Semitic civilization, which would centre on Babylon, further north. In the two millennia which form the historical backdrop to the Old Testament, the specific centres of power would vary, the two key focal points being Babylon and the cities of Assyria (Assur, Nineveh and Calah). These are the powers about which the prophets warned their contemporaries, and which would bring the kingdoms of Israel and Judah to their end in due course.

If Mesopotamia was already an 'old' culture by the Biblical period, so too was that at the other end of the fertile crescent, Egypt. The basis of its growth and success was a rich broad delta at the mouth of the Nile (Lower Egypt), and behind it a long narrow ribbon of fertile land lying on both sides of the river as far as Aswan (Upper Egypt). The 'two Egypts' are thus quite distinct. They were united into a single Kingdom at the beginning of the second millennium, with a capital at Memphis (not far from modern Cairo), at the point where the delta gives way to the valley. The first great flowering of Egyptian culture occurred about the middle of the third millennium BCE, the so-called Old Kingdom, stretching from about 2680-2180 BCE. This was also the Pyramid Age. The greatest pyramid is that of Khufu, from about 2540 BCE, consisting of approximately 2.3 million blocks of stone, weighing on average 2.5 tonnes each. This phenomenal engineering achievement must have taken all of Khufu's reign of twenty-three years to finish. The great periods of the second millennium are known as the Middle Kingdom (about 2134-1786) and the New Kingdom (about 1552-1069). The well-known treasures from the tomb of the fourteenth century pharaoh Tutankhamun, with the wonderful golden mask of the king as their centre-piece, belong in this last period. Egypt's most famous glories seem to be those which celebrated the power of the kings. There were cultural achievements of a high order too, however, not least in literature, with impressive writings from the late third millennium.

By the first millennium BCE, the greatness of Egypt lay largely in the past, though there were periods of revival. Israel's most important connections with Egypt, therefore, are in its formative years, in the late second millennium. But as we shall see, there are important cultural and political links between the people of the Old Testament and this gigantic neighbour too.

Other Nations

Our study has been introduced in this way in order to show that the Old Testament did not come into a 'primitive' world. It was on the contrary a highly sophisticated world, and had been for some time. With Egypt and Mesopotamia we have identified the two major presences in the world of ancient Israel. There were, of course, others. Chief among them, in the early Old Testament period, were perhaps the Hittites, Indo-Europeans who built an impressive empire centred on Anatolia (modern Turkey) from around 1800-1200 BCE. They struggled with Egypt, finally in vain, for dominance in Palestine. They are best known to students of the Old Testament for their political treaties, whose form appears to have been borrowed by certain Old Testament religious texts. The later Old Testament period would bring Persia, Greece and Rome into its pages. But their story must wait.

Besides the great powers, the pages of the Old Testament swarm with the names of other peoples: Syrians, Ammonites, Edomites, Moabites, Canaanites. These were the immediate neighbours of ancient Israel, and though there was typically enmity among these small states, their destinies were somewhat bound together. They were in fact strongly linked culturally. Indeed the principal language of the Old Testament, Hebrew, is closely akin to those of the last four mentioned. The Philistines are a case apart on this canvas, being late 'arrivals' from the eastern Mediterranean, and probably one of the groups known to ancient history as the Sea Peoples, who had a devastating effect on the eastern Mediterranean in the late second millennium. The Philistines probably arrived from Crete, with a highly developed culture of their own, belying their modern reputation!

The Ancient World and the Old Testament

This then is the world in which the Old Testament story is played out. The point is made strikingly in the opening pages of Genesis. The influence of Mesopotamia appears when the Garden of Eden is said to be watered by four great rivers, including the Tigris and Euphrates; the other two are not clearly identifiable, but could be veiled references to the Indus and perhaps the Nile (Gen 2:11-14). Furthermore, Abraham, the ancestor of the Israelite and Arab nations, is said to have originated from Ur, in southern Mesopotamia (Gen 11:31; Josh 24:2). His journey took him to the land of Canaan (Palestine); but it did not end there, for no sooner had he arrived than famine drove him to Egypt for sustenance (Gen 12:10). His journey thus embraced the two great poles of Israel's existence in terms of civilization and culture. Moreover, it foreshadowed in a curious way the 'journey' of the nation of Israel, as we shall see.

The life of Israel was closely bound up with the larger political events, over which it had no control. It was born in a period of loosening Egyptian grip on Palestine, probably in the thirteenth century BCE. Briefly great itself under David and Solomon, its story is a gauge of the rise and fall of greater powers: Assyria, Babylon, Persia, Greece, Rome. This is because Palestine is by its nature disputed territory, neither Mesopotamia nor Egypt, yet important to both for reasons of economics and defence.

The position is illustrated by a famous event. In 701 BCE a great army stood at the gates of Jerusalem, demanding the surrender of city and nation. The occasion was celebrated by Lord Byron in a famous first line:

The Assyrian came down like a wolf on the fold...

The Assyrian was none other than Sennacherib, king of the all-conquering power in the region at the time. Now pursuing a campaign of conquest and expansion in southern Palestine, it had reduced the land of Judah, and only Jerusalem held out. Its commander thundered at the cowed inhabitants gathered on the city-wall: 'Who among all the gods ... have delivered their countries out of my hand, that the LORD should deliver Jerusalem out of my hand?' (2 Kgs 18:35). This was Realpolitik in the language of the day, though religion was a powerful motivating force. Nations were as powerful as their gods, and gods were thirsty for conquest and glory.

The near presence of the great powers strikes the reader of the Old Testament continually. When kings of Israel and Judah are under pressure from an enemy, they look to the empires for possible support (2 Kgs 18:21; 2 Kgs 16:7); ordinary people might flee there for refuge (Jer 41:17-18). When prophets threaten calamity on the nation for failure to keep faith with God, the disaster often takes the form of destruction by a more powerful enemy (Jer 6:22-23). It was not only Israel that suffered, of course, from the ambitions of the mighty, but its neighbours too, the minor players in the political scene of the ancient Near East, such as Moab, Edom and Ammon (Jer 27:1-7). In a world in which war was a regular form of diplomacy, times of stability were a rare gift, and ordinary people often lived in fear of their lives being overwhelmed by forces beyond their control.

Trade

The route from north to south was not only for times of crisis; it bore heavy traffic also in time of peace. There were in fact several routes. The 'super-highway', known as the 'Way of the Sea' (Isa 9:1), began in Egypt, left the Mediterranean coast at Joppa (near modern Tel-Aviv), continued through the pass at Megiddo and wound north of the Sea of Galilee to Damascus. A branch of this broke off at Hazor to go directly north to Anatolia, the land of the Hittites. The other main artery was the King's Highway, which linked Damascus and the Gulf of Aqaba at Elath (modern Eilat), keeping west of the Dead Sea and negotiating the difficult passes and wadis (dry river-channels) of Edom.

The caravans that used these routes surface in the Old Testament occasionally. When Joseph's brothers want to get him out of the way without actually killing him, they sell him to passing merchants, who are coming from the direction of Damascus (via Gilead, north and east of the Sea of Galilee) and heading for Egypt (Gen 37:25). (Their route is not precisely the Way of the Sea, as it takes them a little further west, through Dothan and Shechem, in the central Samarian ridge). The caravans were the juggernauts of the ancient world, permitting international commerce. Imports and exports were as important to economic life then as they are now. Egypt, for example, produced grain and linen, but was poor in olive oil. Iron was introduced by the Philistines and sought by Egypt. There was a traffic in spices from Arabia to Egypt and also via Palestine to points north. Moab was famous for wool. A catalogue of traded goods may be found in Ezek 27:24, with reference to Phoenicia in particular, showing how widespread and varied trade was.

It will be clear, however, that (again, as today) it is hard to draw a line between warlike and strictly peaceable activities, given the possible applications of some of the metal goods. Indeed, the protection that caravans enjoyed was connected with the interests of the powerful protectors. The catalogue of wares also hints at the basic social division between rich and poor that characterized much of ancient life, and that became prevalent in Israel during the time of the monarchy. Trade is often associated in the minds of the prophets (as in the Ezekiel passage, Ezek 27:25-36) with the pride and misuse of wealth which they see as so blameworthy (cf. Jer 6:20).

The story of the Old Testament shows that Israel's location in Palestine was largely a liability, and its destiny was to fall victim more than once to the power of invaders, as we shall see. But our present survey is best concluded with a glimpse of the heyday of its history. While a position on a major trade route was on the whole a dangerous thing, since it made more powerful neighbours all too interested in the territory, it could be an advantage, other factors being favourable, since so much wealth had to pass one's door. This happened just once in Israel's life, in the reign of Solomon. The strength of Solomon was no doubt due to the weakness of others at the time. But he took advantage of his position to create a powerful business empire, his economic astuteness illustrated especially by his profitable trade in Egyptian horses and chariots (1 Kgs 10:28-29). His commercial power was broadly based, however. The Queen of Sheba's celebrated visit was almost certainly less for romance (as the popular imagination would have it) than for the purposes of a trade agreement, the Queen representing the interests of the spice traders of Arabia.

The Land

The Extent of the Land

At the end of his life, having brought the Israelites out of Egypt, Moses stood at the top of Mount Nebo, east of the River Jordan and just north of the Dead Sea. From this vantage point in Moab (modern Jordan), he surveyed the land which God had promised to Abraham, from Dan and Gilead in the north to the southern wilderness, or Negeb (Deut 34:1-3). Even though Moses' 'eye was not dim' (Deut 34:7 [RSV]), he could scarcely have actually seen all this, even on a clear day. Moses might well have glimpsed the Mediterranean gleaming in the west, but the narrative is meant to be a rough description of the extent of the land, rather than a realistic record of what can be seen from Nebo.

The ideal limits of the land conceive it as stretching virtually from Egypt to Mesopotamia (Gen 15:18; Deut 11:24; the 'river of Egypt' in the former passage is probably a wady in the north-eastern Sinai peninsula). A more realistic description is found in Num 34:2-12, which sets the northern boundary at Lebo-Hamath, a city at the source of the Orontes (not Hamath itself, which was further north). Even this implies an area well into northern Syria, and was certainly not typically part of Israelite territory. Under Solomon, apparently, Israel did occupy an area as extensive as this; indeed we are told that he controlled Hamath itself in the north (2 Chr 8:4), and enough of Sinai in the south to control Elath and the routes to Arabia (1 Kgs 9:26). It is interesting, however, that the limits of Moses' view from Nebo stretch only to Dan, effectively northern Galilee, and in the south to the Negeb, or southern wilderness. The popular understanding (ancient and modern) of the length of the land - 'from Dan to Beersheba' (Jdg 20:1) - was in fact closer to the reality for most of the Israelite period in Palestine. Beersheba was about 50 miles south-west of Jerusalem.

While the north-south dimensions were in a sense negotiable, the east-west elevations inevitably made their presence felt in people's lives. A cross-section of the land from the Mediterranean to the Jordan shows dramatic variations, in the south especially. A coastal plain gives way to low hills (the Shephelah, literally 'lowland'), then to the mountains which form the central range of the land in both Samaria and Judah. Jerusalem is perched in these, at about 3,000 feet. Not far east of Jerusalem begins the dizzying plunge into the Jordan valley, a fall of 4,000 feet in the 17 miles to Jericho and the few more to the Dead Sea, an improbable 1,312 feet below sea level at its surface (the sea-bed lies a further 1,300 feet down). The underlying reason for this spectacular gash in the land is a rift valley which extends from Syria to East Africa, reaching its lowest point here.

The east-west division of the land just described does not appear so clearly everywhere, and is less marked in the north. There, the central ridge becomes lower to the west of the Sea of Galilee, and a spur cuts north-west to the Mediterranean at modern Haifa, giving the only cliffs on the Palestine shoreline, and the only natural harbour. The rift valley is also less pronounced, though still a clear feature, the Sea of Galilee being 689 feet below sea level.

A Rich Land?

This was the land that was said to 'flow with milk and honey' (Exod 3:17), and whose wealth was pictured in other vivid ways (Deut 8:7-10), almost as a new Garden of Eden. Such descriptions were intended to contrast with the hard life which the Israelites endured in the wilderness of Sinai before they came into the land. But it will be clear from what has already been said that there must have been sharp variations between its parts in terms of wealth and potential quality of life. When, according to our narratives, the land was divided - in anticipation - by Joshua, and the lots began to fall (Josh 15-19), there must have been some bated breath.

The key was rainfall. Broadly, there was more in the north than the south, and more in the west than the east. North-west is best, and south-east has least. The main influence in the east is of course the rift valley. While Jerusalem, high in the Judean mountains, has an average rainfall of over 500 mm (on some estimates higher than that of London!), just a few miles to the east, as one begins the descent to Jericho, one crosses the rain line, and enters the arid land of the Judean desert.

This is, admittedly, the most dramatic variation, but there were others. Life in the hill-country, whether of Judah or Samaria, was harder than life in the coastal plain, or in the fine land of the plain of Jezreel (Esdraelon) to the north of Megiddo and the Carmel range ('Carmel' itself means 'fruitful'). The Jordan valley too was rich because of the natural irrigation afforded by the river. Where it rises in the north, in the vicinity of Dan, water erupts from the ground over a large area and in vast quantities. Here one seems to be at the source of life itself. (Indeed the New Testament's Caesarea Philippi, located in this area, was also known as Panias, or Banyas, after the god Pan). As the Jordan winds its way south of the Sea of Galilee into the arid Samarian and Judean wildernesses, it creates a ribbon of fertile land on either side. The jewel of this is Jericho, a rich oasis in a barren land, just above the Dead Sea. Good land also lay to the west of the Jordan, in biblical Gilead, where some of the tribes settled (Reuben, Gad, and half of Manasseh).

The land, then, was a mixed prospect. In the hills farmers face a constant struggle with stones, which once cleared have a way of resurfacing (hence the labour required in preparing a vineyard, for example, Isa 5:2). With cities set on hills, furthermore (necessarily, for defensive reasons), the normal routines of life, especially the fetching of water, are a severe discipline. The modern visitor to Israel and Palestine is struck by the difficulty of gaining a living from the hill-country (Judah and Samaria are roughly equivalent to the modern 'West Bank'). Terraced farming and modern irrigation have produced crops in improbable situations. In ancient times there may have been more soil in these areas, because there were probably many more trees to prevent soil erosion. Neverthless, the land did not easily yield its fruit.

The problem for the Israelites was worse because for most of its history it was unable to occupy the most desirable parts. The Philistines, with their iron chariots, held the coastal region from their five city-strongholds (Gaza, Gath, Ekron, Ashdod, Ashkelon). Except for the time of David and Solomon (again!) Israel was largely confined to the hill-country and the Shephelah in the south, though it enjoyed more space from time to time in the north. (Oddly, therefore, the modern map of Israel and Palestine reverses the ancient situation, because the modern Palestinian West Bank corresponds to Israel's ancient heartland, while modern Israel proper hugs the old Philistine coast).

The effect of geography may be seen in a number of Old Testament stories. In the time of Gideon, the farmers of Israel became prey to hordes of nomadic Midianites, who swept in from the eastern desert on their camels and plundered their crops, forcing Israelites out of their best arable land into mountain refuges (Jdg 6:1-6). Gideon's Ophrah enjoyed the wealth of the Valley of Jezreel in the north. The Midianites, however, engulfed the whole land as far as Philistine Gaza. In the same period Samson skirmishes with Philistines from his base in the Shephelah, the western limit of Israelite habitation in the south, making occasional forays and retreating to highland safety (Jdg 16:1-3). David's encounter with Goliath occurs in the Valley of Elah, which leads down from the Judean hill-country to the plain, and is thus in the same disputable territory (1 Sam 17:1-3). On the other hand, when David later flees from Saul he finds refuge in the wilderness of Judah, at En-Gedi, an oasis close to the western shore of the Dead Sea, in an otherwise steep, dangerous and waterless terrain in which pursuit was hard (1 Sam 24:1).

The terrain has also left its mark on the poetry of the Old Testament. The best known Psalm of all (Ps. 23) draws its images from shepherding, one of the staple activities of Israel. In a hard climate and terrain, the shepherd knows the delight of grassy places with refreshing streams (v. 2); he also knows the 'right paths', that is, those that are safe from sudden falls, or wild animals. On the other hand, he sometimes goes through dark and threatening places ('the darkest valley', v. 3 - better known in the traditional translation as 'the valley of the shadow of death'); such valleys one might imagine in the steep defiles of the central ridge, or even the dry ravines of the wilderness. The contrast between life-giving, well-watered places and arid, death-dealing ones is everywhere in the poetry of the Old Testament (see also Jer 14:2-6, for a picture of famine). The 'garden' is an ideal of plenty, rest and well-being, not only in Gen 2 (the Garden of Eden), but also in the Song of Songs, a love-song set in a delightful natural environment.

———— Israelite Society ————

What kind of society was that of ancient Israel, and what did it feel like to belong to it? We cannot give a simple answer to this question, as the shape and conditions of society changed considerably during the Old Testament period. Those historical developments will be the subject of the next chapter. Yet there are certain aspects of life in Israel that can be considered here because they seem to derive from Israel's formative period, and have a certain durability.

Cities

For Israel's earliest period in the land, it is well to put out of mind the concept of nation-state in the modern sense. As we have seen, politics on the grand scale was a matter of major power centres struggling for influence. While populations may know some continuity because of natural boundaries, the idea of recognized international borders has not yet come to its time. When Israel arrived in Palestine, it came to a land of city-states, each with its own king and institutions, enjoying only a relative independence under the protection of the major power of the day. Joshua, it will be recalled, was confronted precisely by cities and kings, sometimes in alliance, as he led the Israelites into the land (Josh 9:1-2). In the Canaanite society which

Israel thus encountered, the city was extremely important, the military, economic and political centre of life.

We have some insights into this situation from non-biblical sources. In 1887, a number of letters written on clay tablets were discovered at el-Amarna, site of ancient Akhetaten, capital of Egypt in the fourteenth century BCE. The letters were written from various kings and administrators in Palestine and Syria to the pharaoh, as Egypt was then the dominant power. Some are begging for help in situations where they are feeling pressure from neighbouring cities; the king of Jerusalem, for example, accuses the king of Gezer of carrying out raids against him, and also of not paying his due tribute to the Egyptian garrison. How far the letters protest loyalty when in fact the kings are pursuing their own designs is not clear; it seems that Egyptian power was weakening at the time, and some city-states, especially in Syria, were already looking cannily to the next order of things.

Some cities were of considerable importance in themselves. Hazor, for example, in what would later be Galilee, was the largest Palestinian city in the biblical period, as can be seen at a glance by looking at the 'tell' (that is, the mound which covers an ancient site). At certain times, Hazor may have exercised political leadership among Canaanite cities.

Excavations have had their most brilliant results, however, at Ugarit on the Phoenician coast (modern Ras-Shamra), evidently an important port. Here in addition to buildings, we also have a large amount of documents, so that a good deal can be pieced together about the life of the city, political, economic and religious. It had two temples (to Baal and Dagan), and a huge palace area covering almost 2.5 acres. There were also a considerable number of spacious homes, indicating a wealthy economy. This was based on maritime trade, which required that the city maintain not only an army but also a permanent navy (a number of stone anchors have been dug up).

Ugarit was a moderately extensive kingdom. At the height of its power, in the fourteenth and thirteenth centuries BCE, it apparently controlled an area of some 1,300 square miles. This incorporated a large number of villages, whose population was engaged in agriculture and dairy farming, the 'breadbasket' therefore of the whole kingdom. Ugarit's impressive culture was apparently destroyed by the Sea Peoples in about 1200 BCE.

While Ugarit has special features, especially its sea trade, it tells us something about larger cities in general. A military, political, religious and economic mix, they had a relationship of mutual dependence with a more or less extensive neighbouring region. In the Old Testament dependent villages are sometimes called, in Hebrew, the 'daughters' of the city (Num 21:25). In times of crisis, this dependence would become strained, as the rural population abandoned their vulnerable dwellings to share the protection of the townsfolks' walls. Thus the normal strains of siege conditions were quickly aggravated, and the well ordered urban life could turn rapidly to chaos.

Tribe and Family

When Israel settled in Canaan there was something of a clash of cultures. The story of Israel's beginnings will be our next concern (see Chapter 2). At this stage we simply notice that while the culture of Canaan was monarchical and centralized, Israel's was essentially tribal and decentralized. That is, it was not a city culture, but a culture based on family and clan. Memories of Israel's fright at the impressive strength of Canaanite cities are preserved in the accounts of their approach to the land (Num 13:28; Deut 1:28). Furthermore, the story of Israel's first entry to the land shows that it is a head-on clash between two different kinds of society. One of the significant things about the grisly account of Israel's destruction of Jericho is that the city is not occupied by the Israelites, but destroyed and condemned never to be resettled (Josh 6:26). Ai too is made 'forever a heap of ruins' (Josh 8:28). It is true that the picture of the conquest also envisages Israel occupying territories with their towns and villages (Josh 15:21-32). And in due course this new arrival in Canaan would adapt largely to the Canaanite city model. In the first instance, though, it is important to understand Israel's tribal character.

The biblical picture is of twelve tribes descended from the patriarch Jacob. The idea of a 'brotherhood' is thus built into the concept of Israel as we have it. This has its cash-value, as it were, in a sense that the tribes in the land belonged somehow together. Whereas in the Canaanite system 'belonging' had more to do with the centralized political reality, in Israel it was based on a shared memory, an understanding of God. Our earliest pictures of Israel in the land bring out this belonging together. Judges 5 is widely acknowledged to be one of the oldest passages in the Old Testament. It is a poem celebrating a military victory won by two 'judges', Deborah and Barak, over a Canaanite power based on the great city of Hazor. The song recalls how certain of the tribes combined forces to bring about the victory (Jdg 5:14-15a, 18). But it also bemoans the failure of some to join in, and this is the telling point (vv. 15b-17). The expectation of concerted effort is clearly there. Israel, then, though it had no king and no centralized authority, could and did act as a concerted whole. As a political arrangement this system is hard to describe or understand. But the cohesion of the tribes, according to the biblical picture, derives from their belonging together as the people of Yahweh, the God who met them in the desert in Sinai.

The tribal system also needs to be understood from within, however. In the Old Testament people are very often introduced by reference to their family and tribe. Saul's father Kish is 'son of Abiel, son of Zeror, son of Becorath, son of Aphiah, a Benjaminite' (1 Sam 9:1). Saul, therefore, is provided with a five-generation genealogy, and also a tribe, Benjamin. This means that identity is experienced in terms of kinship. The social structure is usually described as consisting of three levels, the 'father's house', the clan and the tribe. The first of these is what we might think of as an extended family; the second a larger kinship group, perhaps centred on a number of towns and villages in a locality. And the tribe is the umbrella unit, occupying a considerable territory.

The 'father's house' was the smallest unit of identity. It probably consisted of all the generations descended from a single still-surviving ancestor, and could therefore be fairly large. It had important economic functions, and it was this unit that actually owned land, and was responsible for the subsistence of its members. It may be that brothers continued effectively to share ownership of land even after the death of the father. Its significance extended beyond economics, however, to personal identity. The genealogy of Kish, given above, scarcely implies that the named ancestors of Saul are all still alive. (The long-lived might hope to see four generations; hence 'to the fourth generation' in the Second Commandment, Exod 20:5). Yet it is possible that the oldest people still living would have been born in the lifetime of Aphiah, the most venerable forebear mentioned here. Saul's identity, then, is provided not only by his father and grandfather, but beyond them by a kind of corporate memory in the kinship group. This is the basis of acceptance and belonging in Israelite society.

Next in ascending order of size is the 'kinship group', sometimes alternatively known as the 'clan' (though the latter term is no longer thought appropriate for Israel by anthropologists). This group is an association of the smaller units known as 'father's houses'. Its importance is largely in terms of territorial ownership. This is not to say that the 'kinship group' as such owned land. Rather it implies that it protected land ownership within the group, by means which we shall notice shortly. This means that the kinship group was strongly associated with a geographical location. Thus the names of kinship groups sometimes become synonymous with the names of towns and villages. The famous prophecy concerning a ruler to be born in Bethlehem is a case in point (Mic 5:2) – where Bethlehem is described as a 'clan of Judah'. Similarly, town-names from pre-Israelite Canaan, such as Shechem, Hepher and Tirzah, seem to be adopted in Israel as kinship names (Josh 17:2-6; cf. Gen 34 for Shechem; Josh 12:17, 24). Biblical characters are sometimes introduced with data about their family and tribe, as in the case of Saul (1 Sam 9:1), and sometimes with data about place, as in the case of Gideon (Jdg 6:11) and David (1 Sam 16:1) - though even here the father's name is crucial to identity. And there is other evidence of place-names and personal names being interchangeable (e.g. Machir appears as a place-name in Jdg 5:14, though it occurs first as the name of a grandson of Joseph; Gen 50:23). All this means that kinship identity shades over into place identity.

Some of the most important aspects of Israel's life are to be understood within the framework described. The kinship group's responsibility for property came into play when a family ('father's house') became poor - which might easily happen as a result of a couple of bad harvests. In these cases it could survive by selling property, and ultimately by selling the family itself into slavery. However, these arrangements are not what we would understand by them, but mechanisms for the preservation of the social system. Sale of land was not to be permanent, but a temporary measure, intended as a means of raising money for the owner to tide him over a difficult time. The Old Testament has laws which provide for the return of land to the original owner after a specified period. The basic period was seven years (Deut 15:1-6), with an 'omnibus' restitution after fifty years, the so-called 'jubilee' (Lev 25:8-17). Slavery had in common with land-forfeiture that it was (ideally) voluntary, temporary and intended to put the slave back on his feet (Exod 21:2-3; Deut 15:12-17). The lives of slaves were protected by the law (Exod 21:20), uniquely in the ancient Near East - though it seems that the slave's master enjoyed considerable rights over the slave while he or she was in that condition (Exod 21:4-6, 21).

It is not known whether or how well this system actually worked in Israel, and there is a question about how ancient some of the laws cited are. One recorded case of slave-release occurred in the reign of King Zedekiah of Judah, when the king himself spearheaded a general amnesty of slaves because of the law that we know from Deuteronomy (Jer 34:9-10). Sadly, however, the good intention bore no lasting fruit, and the owners immediately took their slaves back again! (Jer 34:11). The incident probably speaks volumes about the realities of life during the long period of the monarchy. But there is evidence that the kinship group had means apart from the seventh-year restitution by which to retain the land within the group, and to ensure the freedom of people. There were two important devices, namely 'redemption' of property, and the law of levirate marriage, which we know in part both from law and story, as we shall see.

The term 'redemption' has a modern echo in the redeeming of property from the pawnshop. The principle in Old Testament times was not very different, except that it brings in the factor of kinship obligation. If a family had to sell land because of poverty there was an obligation on the nearest kin to 'redeem' it for the group (the law is in Lev 25:25). This might either be a preventive measure, or after the event. The arrangement brought a certain benefit to the redeemer, who would become the effective owner of the land, at least in the short term, the distressed relatives becoming dependent on him (Lev 25:36-41). The identification of the person responsible, the 'kinsman redeemer', presumably had something to do with closeness of relationship and also ability to perform the duty. Jeremiah seems to have been on a mission to do just this for his cousin Hanamel when he was arrested on suspicion of treason during the last siege of Judah (Jer 37:11-13, for the arrest; Jer 32:6-12, for the transaction, successfully made in the end, albeit with Jeremiah in jail, v. 2). The latter passage, incidentally, sheds intriguing light on the legal process surrounding the act, to which we shall return.

The odd practice of 'levirate marriage' is part of the same set of customs. This is the provision that, should a man die without a male child to succeed to his name and property, his brother should marry the widow, in order to have a son who would legally be the dead man's heir (Deut 25:5-6). The brother, evidently, had the right to refuse, perhaps in recognition that he would stand to lose a share in the family property which might now fall to himself and his own children, but if he did he could expect to incur the strong disapproval of the group (Deut 25:7-10). It is not clear how this law relates to that of Lev 18:16, which prohibits sexual intercourse between a man and his sister-in-law (in the context of a comprehensive series of such prohibitions). This can hardly be meant to address a situation in which the woman's husband is still alive, since that would presumably not need separate legislation from the laws against adultery (Exod 20:14; Deut 22:22). If the law of levirate and the laws of prohibited sexual relations were operative at the same time the former can only have been an exception for this particular case.

The function of the law is clear enough, namely to preserve the integrity of the kinship group and its members, and the relationship between it and the inherited land. Admittedly there are aspects of this provision that go deeper than land possession in itself; the idea of perpetuating a person's 'name' was an important element in identity and status. There was also the practical need to care for the widow. But the connection between these things and preventing the land from being inherited by an outsider to the group (by the widow's remarriage) was close.

The story of Ruth provides an indirect commentary on the concepts here. The narrative is a peculiarly feminine one (giving the Hebrew beginner plenty of practice in those awkward feminine grammatical forms of verbs!). It exposes the vulnerable position of women in Israel who had no close male relative. The feminine interest of the story has led some to suggest that its author may have been a woman.

The legal problem in Ruth is posed by the death of the husband and two sons of Naomi, leaving her and her two daughters-in-law bereft. The issue is that Naomi, because of her straitened circumstances on her return from Moab where the family had fled from famine, must sell her deceased husband's land (Ruth 4:3). A kinsman-redeemer is needed, therefore, to keep it in the family. The nearest kin refuses to do it (as he is entitled to), and so Boaz, a little further removed in the family tree, takes on the role. The peculiarity in the story is that Ruth 'comes with the territory' (Ruth 4:5)! The issue in Ruth therefore seems to be a sort of mix of redemption and the levirate law, for here the 'next of kin' (in terms of redemption) is not actually the brother (apparently) of Ruth's deceased husband. The connection between law and narrative, therefore, is not quite as close as we might like, a comment in itself on the complexity of the social system of Israel and our partial knowledge of it. (It may also be a comment on the elusive character of narrative - how can we know that the characters in Ruth are behaving according to extant laws anyway?)

The Process of Law

The practices which we have observed draw our attention to the need in Israel (as everywhere) for due legal process. In the towns of Israel the admininistration of the laws was presided over by the 'elders' (e.g. Deut 21:1-9). The role of 'elder' is based on leadership in the kinship group. There are also 'judges' (e.g. Deut 19:17-18), who were tribal officials (Deut 1:13-16, 16:18-20). Legal processes can be handled at different levels in the tribe. The town, however, is the first place in which disputes were heard, and legal actions typically happened at the city-gate, with a gathering of elders. Evidently there were due and proper ways of proceeding, with rules governing witnessing, both in criminal cases (Deut 19:15-19) and civil. A minimum number of elders may have been required for certain kinds of process (Ruth 4:2). Procedures in civil cases are well illustrated by the narratives about Ruth and Jeremiah, which we have already met. (In Jeremiah's case, the location is his prison, not the city-gate, for unavoidable reasons!). Difficult cases will have involved the tribal officials. There was in addition a superior court, consisting of priests and judges, located at sanctuaries. This will have been resorted to in difficult cases or for solemn undertakings. The law of slave-release in Exodus has an example of this, when it requires that a slave who opts not to accept release be taken 'before God', for a ceremony to establish this decision (Exod 21:6). There seems also to have been a kind of 'High Court' at the central sanctuary of the time (Deut 17:8-9).

How the law-codes related to these processes is not clear. The codes may have been kept at sanctuaries (or the central sanctuary), and studied by experts who advised local judges.

Women and Marriage

It will be clear from the preceding section that the status of women in Old Testament times was not one of strict equality with men. The position of women was obviously bound up with the social structure that we have been observing, in which the responsibilities were apparently entirely in the hands of men; priests must be male, and it seems to be largely taken for granted that elders, teachers, prophets and officials were men also (although there were exceptions, as we shall see in a moment). The legal picture is illustrated by laws governing sexual offences, as in Deut 22:13-30. Here a number of situations are envisaged. The first is the most telling (vv. 13-21). It concerns a situation in which a newly married man believes that his bride was not a virgin before the marriage, a process for establishing the truth or falsehood of his claim, and the dreadful consequences for her if the allegation is upheld – she is stoned to death. The entire process is conducted by men. It is the husband's prerogative to accuse his wife; the elders supervise the legal enquiry, and if the sentence is passed, it is the men of the town who carry out the execution. Moreover, they do so 'at the entrance of her father's house' (v. 21). The last point is important, because it implies that the punishment bears very closely on the father. This was certainly the case, because the marriage was understood as an agreement between the father of the bride, to whom she had hitherto 'belonged', and the new husband, to whom she would henceforth 'belong'. The punishment at the door of the father's house was a kind of demonstration that the agreement between the two men had effectively been broken by the father.

The concepts behind these practices arise from the nature of the society which we have begun to observe. They have to do with the need to ensure offspring for the family. This has an economic aspect, since a household needed to count on the next generation taking on the labour of the land. Marriage, consequently, was an economic arrangement. This is clear from the law in Deut 22:28-29, where a man rapes a virgin, and when discovered, has to pay compensation to the father, as well as marrying the woman. He has to marry her because she has now become otherwise unmarriageable. And he has to pay the father because he has robbed him of the bride-price which he would otherwise have been able to expect for her. The commandment which prohibits adultery (Exod 20:14) is concerned partly with these factors, since adultery involves a kind of robbery.

The picture just given must be qualified. After all, it can be said that there is an economic aspect to marriage in all societies, including modern ones. And plainly the Old Testament knows about romantic love too (think of Jacob and Rachel, and the exquisite Song of Songs). Moreover, the real influence of women in society was almost certainly much greater than appears from a study of the legalities. Among powerful Old Testament women is Deborah, who was both judge and prophet (Jdg 4-5). And there were plainly other female prophets (2 Kgs 22:14). They appear to have had a role in the education of children (Prov 10:1), and could expect obedience from them just as the father might (Deut 21:18). They are likely to have had a good deal of real power in the administration of households.

Nevertheless, many modern writers on the Old Testament feel that the picture of the place of women is negative, and therefore that it is not easy for women to find it relevant or affirming. Such writers, who include, of course, a large number of women, bear the name, rightly or wrongly, of 'feminist'. They are exploring new ways of making this 'patriarchal' book accessible to women. But we must leave further consideration of their work until a later point in our study.

—— Religion in the Ancient World ——

We have seen that the societies of Israel and Canaan were rather different. Israel's tribally based society entered a land which was dominated by the city culture of Canaan. In practice, Israelites too dwelt in towns and villages from early in their life in the land, and became a settled people, living from agriculture. A visitor might scarcely have noticed the difference between Canaanites and Israelites, at least at a superficial glance. Yet there were profound differences between the two - at least inasfar as Israelites were faithful to the religion of their ancestors. And these differences were fundamentally religious. Israel's religion has to be put in a broader context than simply that of Canaan, however, for there were certain similarities in religion throughout the ancient Near East, especially between Canaan and Mesopotamia. It is important, therefore, to give some account of religion in the world of the Old Testament. Our next observations are based primarily on Mesopotamia and Canaan, but we shall come finally to Egypt.

Basic Concepts

Some of the most impressive buildings in early times were religious ones. The 'ziggurats' of Ur and other cities of the Sumerians and later Babylonians were temple-towers whose tops were thought to reach to heaven - hence the Old Testament's scornful story of the Tower of Babel (Gen 11:1-11). These great sanctuaries were considered to be meeting places between heaven and earth. Similar 'mythological' concepts lay behind all ancient temples. That is, they were not simply places where people came together to worship, but they somehow symbolized the dwelling place of God (or the god) in heaven (temples were typically dedicated to a particular god). At the same time, they represented the presence of God (or the god) on earth.

The temples were manifestations of people's natural religious sensitivities. The awe of early people before the powerful forces around them is evident from their writings. Their religion was a way of understanding and ordering the world in which they lived. The god took care of their needs in terms of the fertility of the land, and also of protection from enemies. And they paid due attention to his, or her,

— 24 —

service. Temples were attended by special personnel, namely priests, and in some cases priestesses. They carried out due rituals, such as the sacrifices of animals, and the offering of gifts brought by the people.

It sometimes seems from our texts that people had a somewhat crude idea of the presence of the god: the sacrifices can be understood as food for the god, and libations (or drink-offerings) his drink. This was all part of ensuring his or her favour, and thus maintaining order in the world. In the face of the unpredictable element in human affairs, people obviously did not imagine that the god could or would always do what they wanted. There could be rivalries in heaven. The Babylonian flood, for example, was decreed by Ellil, whose plan to destroy all humanity was foiled by Ea, who happened to be well disposed towards Utnapishtim, the Babylonian 'Noah'. Gods had temperaments and limitations, they had whims and got irritated. In these circumstances, they had to be persuaded by all means. Sacrifices are part of this mentality. But there were other methods. Ritual prostitution, for example, involving specially designated cult-prostitutes and often the king, was a method of trying to ensure fertility of ground and body, because of the special kind of symbolic logic that existed in the religion. The most extreme method of persuading the god was by the sacrifice of children, associated especially with the little-known god Molech, a practice forbidden and abhorred in Israel (Lev 20:2-5; Deut 12:31), though sometimes practised nevertheless (2 Kgs 21:6), and certainly resorted to by others (2 Kgs 3:27). A famous archaeological find in the sanctuary of Tanit at ancient Carthage (a culture related to that of Phoenicia on the shoreline to the north of Palestine) uncovered the bones of children.

Religion and the State

Mesopotamia

We have so far seen that in the millennium or so before the biblical period powerful states grew up in the region. What we did not observe, except indirectly, was that these states had very strong official religions. Indeed it is impossible to conceive of them aside from religion. While it is true, therefore, that the religion of ancient people answered to deep human needs, it was also highly political. The temples in the great cities declared that the god was present there.

The point is illustrated in the epic of creation that we know from Babylon. Its precise origins are unclear; the classic epic comes from

Babylon in the mid-second millennium BCE, but parts of it may be even older. It tells of the origins of the universe, from a watery Chaos to the world as it was known. The Chaos was symbolized by a great monster, Tiamat, who together with her 'husband' Apsu, were the first gods. Together they gave birth to the other gods (this story is therefore a 'theogony', a 'birth of the gods'). Apsu is in due course killed by one of the gods (Ea), and the others, led by Marduk, rebel against Tiamat. Marduk kills Tiamat, and from her carcass creates the world. In this way order is created out of disorder, which had been symbolized by Tiamat. Marduk then also creates human beings from the blood of the god Kingu, an accomplice of Tiamat, condemning them to labour for ever for the benefit of the gods. Finally, he establishes himself as the high god in his temple Esagila in Babylon.

There is a close link between this epic and the worship in Babylon. It was recited annually at the so-called Akitu festival, a 'New Year' celebration, originally in the autumn but later held in the spring. The purpose of this festival was purification and atonement, the king himself enduring atonement rituals on behalf of his people.

The creation account, therefore, is a powerful political tool establishing the supremacy of Babylon. There were, however, local variations - in Assyria, the same epic was told with the high god Assur substituted for Marduk! There were other variations too. In Assyria the relationship between the god and the king took on particular military implications. By the early part of the first millennium, the god Assur had become purely an imperial god, that is, he was exclusively concerned with the expansion of the empire. This explains, or at least legitimates, the actual expansion of Assyria in the area after about 900 BCE; the great conquering kings of the Assyrians were acting at the behest of the god. After conquests, kings would take throne-names which in effect boasted about the extent of their power, such as 'king of the four boundaries of the world'.

The military aspect of religion – or the religious aspect of war – is perhaps most clearly illustrated in Assyria. Wars in general, however, were essentially religious, conducted in the belief that the nation's god was superior to other gods. This was why, when nations made captives, they sometimes symbolically took the 'god' captive, that is, they captured the idol of the god of the defeated people, and publicly carried it off as part of the triumphal procession. There are echoes of this practice in the Old Testament (Jer 48:7).

The mix of religious belief, worship and politics gives some insight into what students of the Old Testament call myth. The myth is the undergirding belief about the world order. It is sustained in religion, worship, and literature, and it explains and reinforces an understanding of a particular people's place in the world.

The king's relationship with the high god was such that the king himself could sometimes be thought of as 'divine'. Some Mesopotamian kings, such as Naram-Sin of Akkad, 2250-2213 BCE, had the term 'god' set before their names. This was the exception rather than the rule, however, kings normally being seen as mere mortals. However, in one special context kings were considered to become 'divine', namely in a religious ceremony known as the 'sacred marriage', in which the king represented Dumuzi, the god of fertility, and a high priestess took the role of Ishtar, the goddess of love. After the ritual consummation of the 'marriage', the king was considered a god. The practice was found among the Sumerian kings, and their successors in Babylon in the early first millennium, until stopped by the great lawgiver Hammurapi in the eighteenth/seventeenth centuries.

Canaan

The immediate religious background to the Old Testament is furnished by the religion of Canaan. The chief god there was El, whose name is also known from the Old Testament itself, as it was used by Israel's ancestors, the 'patriarchs' Abraham, Isaac and Jacob (Gen 21:33; 31:13). El, however, seems to have had less impact in practice on people's lives and thinking than Baal, the storm-god, also known as Hadad, and very familiar to readers of the Old Testament. (Queen Jezebel, the Phoenician wife of Israel's King Ahab, brought 450 of her prophets of Baal to the Israelite capital Samaria; 1 Kgs 18:22). As the ruler of the elements, Baal ensured fertility and therefore life. There were important goddesses too. Anat was Baal's consort. Asherah (the consort of El) was also prominent, as we know from the commands in the Old Testament to destroy images of her (Exod 34:13). And another female deity, Ashtaroth, is the Canaanite (and biblical) equivalent of the Babylonian Ishtar (Jdg 2:13; 10:6). There were other deities too. And the popularity of Canaanite deities in Palestine has been demonstrated by the discovery of a large number of small images (figurines) at various sites, presumably representing gods and goddesses.

Our knowledge of Canaanite religion has been greatly improved by the discovery of texts from Ugarit. The most important concern Baal directly, being epic tales of his victories over other heavenly powers. In one of these he confronts the god Yam, or 'Sea' (*yam* means 'sea' in both Ugaritic Canaanite and Hebrew). Yam is both the primeval watery Chaos and a great sea monster. The struggle between Baal and

Yam seems to be the Canaanite counterpart of the Babylonian conflict between Marduk and Tiamat, the issue in both cases being the order and stability of the world. A second narrative tells how, after his victory, Baal takes his place in a palace, thus establishing his rule in the heavens. At the same time, this becomes the foundation myth of the temple of Baal on Mount Zaphon in Syria, located 25-30 miles north of Ugarit.

The Baal cycle is complete with the story of another great conflict, now between Baal and the god Mot, or Death. This epic is remarkable for the fact that Baal is at first defeated. The power of evil and death overcomes the power of order and good. Baal even descends into the underworld, and is powerless to return. All is not lost, however, for he is rescued by his consort Anat, who first slaughters Mot in a bloody contest. The story may have related to the experience of the seasons, where winter regularly brings 'death' to the natural order, and this is symbolized by Baal's sojourn in the underworld. Yet this cannot be the whole story, for it also suggests the fine balance in the order of things between good and evil, the defeat of Baal expressing how fragile existence was. There is a good deal of foreboding and fear in these stories.

It is possible that all these stories had their home in worship, perhaps an annual New Year festival. If so, there would be further echoes of Mesopotamia, although there is less evidence of this for Canaan. We do not know what role Canaanite kings might have played in such ceremonies. But we do know from other texts (notably Keret, the story of a king's need to marry and have a successor), that here too the role of the king was religious. He had a special relationship with the god, or high god, and on his well-being depended that of the people.

Egypt

In Egypt, religion took distinctive forms. The sun played a major part in the Egyptian idea of God. The sun-god was Re', although the sun could also be worshipped as Atum. Creation was conceived differently from Mesopotamia, there was apparently no primeval conflict between powers of good and evil. Indeed Creation does not seem to have been an act. Rather 'the creator (i.e. sun-God) emerged spontaneously out of the void before time and before matter' (Quirke, 23) – though there is a similarity with Mesopotamia in the fact that this primeval void is imagined as an infinite expanse of waters, known as Nun. Water obviously played an immense part in Egyptian psychology, with the Nile at the heart of it. The annual Nile flood, in fact, was characterized as the god Hapy, and seen as a renewal of creation.

There is a certain awe at the grandeur of creation in the strange imagery in Egyptian depictions of deity. The use of animals and birds, such as the falcon, is highly symbolic. Re' is depicted enthroned with a human body and a falcon head, the latter expressing divine power. The sphinx is an image of a king, the lion's body symbolizing power. There were also actual animal representations of gods. Sacred bulls were virtually worshipped at some of the great sanctuaries. The most famous was the Apis bull at Memphis, which was a kind of embodiment of the god Ptah. Such bulls were regarded with tremendous awe, offerings were made to them and they enjoyed pampered lives. They were not gods themselves, it should be said, but symbolized the presence of the god on earth.

Egyptian religion, though by no means a unified thing, sometimes tried to express the relationship between gods and the world in a theological system. One important attempt is known as the Heliopolitan theology, with a grouping of nine gods (the Heliopolitan Ennead), Re' at its head. The gods in this construct bore a close relationship to the natural order. For example, directly below Re' are Shu and Tefnut, forming a pair of opposites: Shu represents dryness, Tefnut moisture. These are further linked to concepts of order and disorder, which are fundamental to the whole divine genealogy.

Egyptian theology, like Mesopotamian, can resort to narrative to express profound things. The basic conflict between order and disorder is played out in one such narrative, in which Osiris represents life and order, while Seth stands for destruction and violence. Osiris is killed by Seth, only to be brought back to life by his sister Isis. The basic elements here recall the death of Baal and his 'resurrection' through his sister and consort Anat. There is a further similarity between the Egyptian and Canaanite stories, since in both there is a connection with fertility. Egypt puts its own slant on the conflict between life and death, however, by making Osiris the god of the 'blessed dead', and associating him with the process of mummification. (There may even be a distant echo of the Old Testament's Seth in the Egyptian figure, since the biblical Seth features in a story of a first murder, and the life beyond it [Gen 4]. The details of the stories, and the characters, are vastly different, however).

The many gods in Egypt, were often associated with particular places. Thus Re' was worshipped at Iunu, Ptah at Memphis and Amun at Thebes - the 'hidden one', worshipped by priests in a cult that was hidden from public view in a great temple. There do not seem to have been clear lines of distinction between gods. Indeed they could even fuse together, and an important such fusion did occur between Re' and Amun. In the second millennium Amun of Thebes was effectively the state-god. Fused with Re' he became Amun-Re', and as such an imperial god, who sanctioned military expansion, rather as later in Assyria.

There was a close relationship between the king and deity. Indeed it was so close that kingship could be represented in the same way as a god, for example by a falcon. It was a short step from this to the idea that the pharaoh was actually a god. Such an idea underlies the concept of the pyramid, a tomb that pointed to heaven. Khufu's pyramid was not only a stupendous feat of engineering. It was also a monument fit for a god. If Mesopotamian kings hesitated to think of themselves as divine, there were no such inhibitions among the pharaohs of the older Egyptian kingdoms.

There were a number of important religious themes in Egyptian religion. Religion could be personal. This seems clear from certain personal names of people. 'Padiamun', for example, means 'the man given by Amun'. There was also a belief in the personal survival of death. A famous picture shows the departed soul before the judgment throne of Osiris, the god of the blessed dead, his good and bad deeds being weighed in scales. The survival of death is not a theme in other ancient Near Eastern religion, and only marginally in the Old Testament. Yet we have seen that personal religion is not the whole story; religion could also be highly political.

The transcendent power of God is another important emphasis. This is caught in the idea of the god as the sun, for example. It contrasts, however, with the belief that the god could be present on earth, as illustrated by the sacred bulls of Memphis and other places. That contrast actually comes to expression in one important combination of two gods, Re' and Horus (as Ra'-Horakhty).

A revolution occurred in the fourteenth century (about 1375 BCE). At this time, religion in Egypt had become very political, with different temples and their priesthoods rivalling the pharaoh for power. The change was brought about by Pharaoh Amen-hotep IV, who changed his name to Akh-en-Aton, thus declaring himself the worshipper of Aton, the 'sun-disc', and rejecting other gods. He regarded him as the one universal god, calling him 'the sole god, like whom there is no other' - and thus may be considered the first monotheist. Actively opposing the older religion, he moved his capital to El-Amarna, and devoted himself to his new ideas, and to art and literature. The move also brought with it the collapse of the powerful priestly aristocracy. Akh-en-Aton's monotheism may seem to be a parallel to that of the Old Testament. In fact the two concepts are quite different, the Egyptian being much more theoretical, whereas the Old Testament's understanding bears directly on human life (see below, Chapter 6).

———— Religion: conclusion ————

These brief accounts show how dangerous it is to generalize about religion in the Old Testament world. While there were certain continuities, it varied from nation to nation, and even within nations. Religion was a powerful force in people's minds, and had many aspects. It was essentially a way of trying to understand the universe, and it could be very subtle. The capacity for change within religion, and the dialogue between important themes, shows the danger of regarding ancient religion - or non-biblical religion - as by definition 'primitive'.

The world of Mesopotamia, Egypt and Canaan is the world of the Old Testament. Viewed from one perspective, Israel is a minor state among major powers. It stood alongside other minor players, such as Moab, Ammon, Syria, Edom, which made relatively little impact on the world of their day and which have left little legacy behind. To an Assyrian or an Egyptian, Yahweh the god of Israel, was no more significant than Chemosh the god of Moab or Milcom the god of Ammon. He, and it, were just part of the big mix that was ancient religion. And we shall indeed meet many aspects of that religious mix on the pages of the Old Testament. On the material side, there was much in common between Israel and Canaan (sacrifices, priests, temple, feasts etc.). And at the level of ideas, there are similarities also: creation, personal religion, national religion, destiny, salvation, the God of power and the God who is close. Other nations wrestled with these things.

Yet history has marked out the religion of Israel. In its imageless monotheism, it was scandalously different from other religions (the Romans would call the Jews 'atheists'!). And it was Israel and her God whose history produced the three great monotheisic religions. We shall get a better idea why this was so as we continue first with the history of Israel in the Old Testament period, then with a study of its literature and ideas.

Further Reading

General:

J. Rogerson and P. Davies, *The Old Testament World*, Cambridge University Press, 1989

J. J Bimson, *The World of the Old Testament*, scripture Union, London, 1988

R. de Vaux, *Ancient Israel: its Life and Institutions*, Darton, Longman and Todd, London, 1961

Other:

J. B. Pritchard, *Ancient Near Eastern Texts*, Princeton University Press, 1969 (a standard anthology, often abbreviated to *ANET*)

W. von Soden, *The Ancient Orient: an Introduction to the Study of the Ancient Near East*, Eerdmans, Grand Rapids, 1994

S. Dalley, *Myths from Mesopotamia,* OUP, 1989

J. Day, *Molech: a God of Human Sacrifice in the Old Testament*, Cambridge University Press, 1989

J. C. L. Gibson, *Canaanite Myths and Legends*, T. & T. Clark, Edinburgh, 1978 (second edition)

Stephen Quirke, *Ancient Egyptian Religion*, British Museum, London, 1992

Miriam Lichtheim, *Ancient Egyptian Literature I, II,* University of California, Berkeley, 1973, 1976

C. J. H. Wright, *God's People in God's Land*, Eerdmans/ Paternoster, Grand Rapids/Carlisle, 1990

2

OLD TESTAMENT HISTORY

Introduction

We have seen something of the world in which the people of the Old Testament lived, moved and had their being. We shall find as we proceed that an understanding of that world affects every other aspect of our study. The next important angle on our subject is what we might call Old Testament history. It is important to understand what is meant by this: that is, what kind of 'historical' knowledge can we have, and what kind is actually important for our subject? To some extent, we must think like historians here: we consider and evaluate sources, including the Bible itself, and try to understand what actually happened in the history of the people called Israel. In doing so, however, we remember that our subject is the 'Old Testament', or the 'Bible'; that is, we have taken as our subject a body of literature that is by its nature religious. Our interest is therefore different from that of the historian as such, because we shall ask also about the religious history reflected in our texts, that is, a kind of history of ideas. This is why I have chosen to define the present topic as Old Testament History rather than the History of Israel, although the two concepts are related. It will bring us close to the 'theology' of the Old Testament, although strictly that is something different again, which we shall return to at a later point.

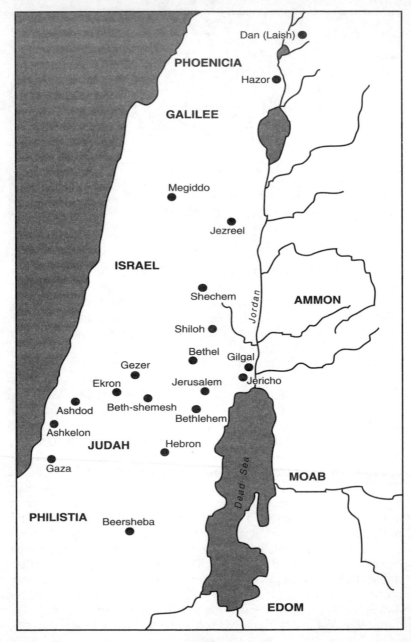

Beginnings

The first question is where to begin. We shall leave aside at this point what is called the 'primeval history', namely Genesis 1-11, because that will come more naturally later, for reasons which we shall see. The first part of the Old Testament story concerns the 'patriarchs', or forbears, of Israel. These are Abraham, Isaac, Jacob (father, son and grandson), and the twelve sons of Jacob (Joseph, Judah, Benjamin and the rest), who give names to the twelve tribes.

Their story is told in Genesis 12-50. Writers on the Old Testament take different views about whether these narratives are really part of the 'history' of its people. Indeed while some standard studies of the History of Israel (such as that of John Bright) include the patriarchs and write about a patriarchal 'period', others (such as that of Martin Noth) do not, but begin with the period of the judges.

The historical problem is simply that there is no evidence apart from the biblical stories for the existence of the patriarchs. Furthermore, some scholarly thinking about the Old Testament considers the stories as creations of a later age, providing an explanation of the nation's origins. On the other hand, it is not entirely surprising that Abraham should have left no firm clues to his historicity behind him. The patriarchal story is essentially a family history. People who live in tents and who move around with their households do not leave material evidence for archaeologists to recover.

There are general reasons for thinking that there was indeed a patriarchal period. These have to do with what we know of the world of the time, which we have begun to examine in the previous chapter. If we try to link in the family history of Abraham, Isaac and Jacob with the subsequent Old Testament story, a time has to be supposed for them in the early to middle second millennium BCE. This is because we have to reckon back from a date widely adopted for the exodus of the Israelites from Egypt, namely the mid-thirteenth century BCE. This date itself is not fixed and certain, however, and therefore there are very large variables in any discussion of a patriarchal period. Possible parameters for it are about 2000-1500 BCE.

Historical 'fixes' on it take two main forms. The first depends on how well the 'world' of the patriarchs, as far as we can know it from the biblical narratives, matches the world of the second millennium. Very generally, Abraham's journey fits with that world. He sets out with his father Terah from Ur (which we can reasonably take to mean the ancient Sumeran city in southern Mesopotamia), and proceeds round

Time Chart

BCE	Egypt	Canaan	Syria and Mesopotamia
1800			
		The period of the patriarchs	Mari destroyed
1700			
1600			Nuzu (in Mesopotamia)
1500			
1400	Akhenaten	Amarna period	
1300	Rameses II Exodus Merneptah	Philistine invasion	Ugarit destroyed
1200	Rameses III Defeat of the Sea	Period of the Judges	
1150	Peoples	Deborah	
1100			
1050		Samuel Saul	
1000	Egypt's power diminishes	David	
950	Pharaoh Shishak	Solomon The kingdom divides	The rise to power of Assyria

Israel, Judah and the rise of Assyria

	Judah	Israel	Syria	Assyria
	Rehoboam	Jeroboam		
	Abijah			
900	Asa	Nadab Baasha Elah Zimri/Tibni	Ben-Hadad I	Shalmaneser III

	Judah	Israel		Assyria/Syria
850	Jehosaphat	Omri Ahab *Elijah*	Ben- Haddad II	
	Ahaziah Athaliah Joash	Ahaziah Joram Jehu	Hazael	
800	Amaziah	Jehoahaz Joash Jeroboam II *Amos*		Adad-nirari III
	Azariah	*Hosea* Zechariah		
750	Jotham Ahaz *Isaiah*	Shallum Menahem Pekahiah The Syro- Ephraimite war	Rezin	Tiglath-pileser III Shalmeneser V
700	*Micah* Hezekiah Manasseh	Hoshea The fall of Samaria (722)		Sargon II Sennacherib Esarhaddon

650 - 300 BCE

	Judah	Babylon	Media
650	Amon / Josiah /*Jeremiah* *Zephaniah / Habakkuk*	(Assyria - the fall of Nineveh)	
600	Nahum /Jehoahaz Jehoiakim / Jehoiachin First deportation Zedekiah	Nebuchadnezzar II *Ezekiel*	
550	Fall of Jerusalem second deportation Gedaliah	Evil-merodach *Deutero-Isaiah* Nabonidus The fall of Babylon	Cyrus II Edict of Cyrus (538) Cambyses II Darius I
500	Some Jews return Zerubbabel Rebuilding of the temple *Haggai / Zechariah*		Xerxes I
450	Ezra Nehemiah		Artaxerxes I Darius II Artaxerxes II Artaxerxes III
400			
350			Fall of the Persian Empire.

333 Alexander the Great: the beginning of Greek rule

the 'fertile crescent' into Canaan and Egypt (Gen 11:31-12:20). Whether the journey of his father Terah had anything to do with the changes that occurred in Ur with the decline of Sumerian power at the beginning of the second millennium we can only speculate. The situation in Palestine itself is apparently one of a mixed population, with no sign of upheaval or enmity. On Sarah's death, Abraham buys a piece of land for her grave from one 'Ephron the Hittite' (Gen 23) - a name which may link him with the Hittites of the powerful kingdom to the north in Anatolia. He himself holds a position of respect among the Canaanite population (Gen 23:6), and even joins a number of their city-kings in a defensive action against foreign invaders (Gen 14). These glimpses of the politics and society of the time are tantalizing, and these are difficult historical questions about the incidents. But the picture is not out of keeping with what we know of the second millennium, with a number of city-kingdoms co-existing more or less peacefully (even if there were strains by the Amarna period, as we have seen).

Social customs have provided a special kind of window on to the patriarchs' world. For example, when Abraham picks out his eldest son Isaac for special privileges (Gen 25:5-6), or when Esau, as Isaac's eldest, is in line for a major share of the inheritance (his 'birthright'; Gen 25:32-34), this custom resembles what seems to have been the case at the Mesopotamian city of Nuzi in the fifteenth century BCE. Abraham's proposed 'adoption' of his slave Eliezer (Gen 15:2-3) is another case in point. It should be said that scholars are divided on whether such parallels are really significant, whether the similarities are really close enough, and whether customs can be regarded as specific to a period.

The second 'fix' on the patriarchal period arises from the biblical text itself. It is clear from our narratives that the religion of the patriarchs is different from the religion that we find in Israel's later history. For example, there is no central place of worship, and no organized priesthood or sacrificial system; instead the heads of families build altars where they wish, and effectively act as priests (Gen 13:18). Specifically, there is little evidence that Jerusalem was important to Abraham, Isaac and Jacob, as it was from the time of David. Other places, such as Hebron (Mamre) and Bethel, are more significant (Gen 18:1; 35:1). This is a very important indication that the patriarchs do indeed represent a distinctive phase in Old Testament history.

Most importantly, they know God as El, which as we have seen is the name of the Canaanite high god. The point can be obscured by the form of the stories in the Old Testament, for there the name

Yahweh (or the LORD) is often used (24:3). However, we are told in the book of Exodus that Abraham, Isaac and Jacob did not know the name Yahweh (Exod 6:3). It is probable, in fact, that the frequent use of that name in Genesis is a result of a re-presentation of the patriarchal stories in a time later than theirs, using the typical Israelite name which would have made sense to the later audience. The patriarchs themselves, however, probably did not use it. (A complicated discussion about the way in which biblical traditions were preserved, and the biblical books written, lies behind this point, and we shall have to consider it separately later.)

On the other hand a number of texts show that the patriarchs knew God as El. It is clearest in the Jacob narratives. Late in his life, when God speaks to Jacob (or 'Israel'), he says: 'I am God, the god of your father'. The first word for 'God' is El (or strictly ha-El, with the definite article), and the second the more usual general word for God (elohim). So we could translate: 'I am El, the god of your father'. On a previous occasion Jacob had built an altar and called it El-Elohe-Israel, or El, the god of Israel (Gen 33:20). (See also Gen 35:1, 3, 7, 11; and compare Gen 17:1 with Exod 6:3). In fact the name El comes in the narratives in a number of combinations (such as El-Shaddai, or God Almighty), which somehow qualify the name. But it seems inescapable that the forbears of Israel are here depicted using the name of the chief Canaanite deity.

The point is not surprising in itself. The Old Testament tells us that Abraham originated in Mesopotamia, where he would have been part of the polytheistic religion of that land (Josh 24:2). In his travels west he would have become familiar with El and the religion of Canaan. The story of Abraham is one of an encounter with the God who is known to the reader of the Bible as the one God (Gen 12:1-3). But this was a new experience to Abraham which he would have had to understand first in terms of his own religious background and concepts, and whose implications he can hardly have grasped all at once. The story of the patriarchs, therefore, is of an encounter with 'Yahweh' (not yet known by name) in the midst of Canaanite religion and ideas.

One of the most interesting texts in this regard is Genesis 14:18-24, where the mysterious Melchizedek enters the story.

Melchizedek appears as the priest-king of the Canaanite city of Salem - the first appearance, albeit cryptic, of Jerusalem in the biblical story (see Ps. 76:2). Our text presents Abraham as equating El (here called El-Elyon, God Most High) with the God whom he now knows, and calling him Yahweh (Gen 14:22)! It is likely that the introduction of the name Yahweh is a later addition to the text. Nevertheless, the story illustrates what seems to have been the major religious issue when Israelites and their forbears trod Canaanite soil - how to understand their own experience of their God Yahweh in relation to the religion of their Canaanite neighbours. This being so, it is too simple to say just that the ancestors of Israel worshipped the Canaanite El. Their understanding of who God was must have been formed by their own experience, even though they used the name familiar from their environment. The religious question here is complex, and perhaps not unlike modern issues that face people of different religions when they try to speak of God together.

——————— Egypt, Exodus, Sinai ———————

The story of Israel in Egypt is one of the most colourful and memorable phases of the account of Old Testament history. The link between the patriarchs and the arrival of a recognizable people of Israel is provided by the story of Joseph, celebrated in the retelling from the Qur'an to Thomas Mann and Andrew Lloyd Webber! The regency of Joseph as vizier in Egypt is not supported by definite evidence outside the Bible, though it has been thought to fit possibly in the Hyksos period in Egypt's history, the Hyksos being a Semitic dynasty of pharaohs (1700-1580). The 'colour' of the story, however, evokes aspects of what we know of the exercise of power in ancient Egypt, though these should not be pressed as firm historical evidence. (There is an interesting example of absolute power delegated to a servant, for example, in the tomb-inscription known as the Autobiography of Weni, a vizier of the late third millennium. Second millennium inscriptions extol the virtues of a good servant in ways which echo the wisdom and justice of Joseph).

The historical issue in Egypt, as quickly appears from the story in Exodus, is the increasing numbers of the people of Israel (Exod 1:7-10). Settled in Goshen, in the eastern delta region, they are quickly reduced to the status of slaves after the death of Joseph because of the threat they are perceived to pose to Egypt. Their assignment to the store-cities of Pithom and Rameses is in keeping with the tremendous investment of human labour needed to manage the vast projects of ancient Egypt. The cities in question were in the delta region (the Septuagint, or Greek translation of the Old Testament, adds On [Heliopolis], the centre of the cult of Re', to the two mentioned here).

Great building projects are known to have been undertaken in the thirteenth century, the 'Ramesside' period, and Israel's slavery could belong to that setting.

This development leads inevitably into the well-known conflict between Moses and Pharaoh, in which Moses demands freedom for God's people and Pharaoh repeatedly refuses, despite wavering several times because of the series of 'plagues' sent by Yahweh. The issue is couched in religious terms, as a demand by Yahweh that Pharaoh should allow the people to leave in order to worship him (Exod 8:1). The climax is the Passover, the defining moment of Israel's history in the Bible, as in Judaism ever since (Exod. 12-13). This final 'plague' - bringing the death of all the firstborn in the land – at last breaks Pharaoh's resistance, and the miraculous 'exodus' of the people from Egypt ensues (Exod 14-15). The sea that is crossed is best understood as the 'Reed Sea' (Exod 13:18), and is presumably a body of water in the eastern delta region, rather than the Red Sea proper, which on any sensible estimate of the route of the exodus would take Israel well out of its way.

With these events we are not yet at the stage of Israel's history when we can verify the reports by means of non-biblical evidence. Only general background points can be made. The date of the exodus is most commonly put in the reign of Rameses II (1290-1224), although a considerably earlier date in the reign of Pharaoh Thutmosis III (1490-1437) is also defended by some scholars. The historicity of the exodus itself is viewed variously; it is both a matter of how one thinks God may have acted in history, and of how one sees the nature of the texts. Gerhard von Rad, one of the most influential writers on the Old Testament in the twentieth century, thought that the story of the exodus was essentially an expression of Israel's faith, rather than actual history. On this view, the events behind the story are largely beyond the scope of the historian to discover. However, it is very likely that a real experience of deliverance from Egypt underlies the narrative, for otherwise it would be hard to explain the central importance which the memory of the exodus has in the Old Testament. And this assumption has been made by a large number of modern critical scholars. (Once again, we must return to fundamental questions about the composition of the Old Testament in their due place).

The leaving of Egypt is not just a departure but it also has a destination. That destination is more than a place, for it involves the people's relationship with Yahweh. It is no accident that it is at this stage of the story that he reveals himself to the people more fully, by giving them his name (Exod 3:12-15). The name itself, mysterious though it appears, implies his commitment to them. At the beginning of their life as a nation, Yahweh is 'with' them (3:12).

This relationship is cemented at Mount Sinai, the 'summit', if we may put it so, of the story of Yahweh and Israel. The narrative is contained in Exodus 19-24. Here the oppressed slaves receive their charter as a nation, a free people; 'Israel' is constituted, and walks the pages of history along with the rest. The instrument that makes them such is a 'covenant' (Exod 19:5). We have seen that covenants, or in the political realm treaties, were part and parcel of the making of relationships in the ancient Near East. Now Yahweh uses the language and concepts of covenant to describe the relationship between him and his people. The essential ingredients are the commitment already shown to them by him in the exodus itself (Exod 19:4), and the commitment required from them in return (Exod 19:8). The Ten Commandments and the laws that follow (Exod 20-23) spell out the conditions of the covenant in detail. The remarkable thing about this covenant is that it substitutes the lordship of Yahweh for the overlordship of a political regime (Egypt). The events reported in Exodus are not simply the story of a 'great escape', but of the creation of a certain kind of people, the decentralized, egalitarian society which we have already described. The crucial thing is that Yahweh is this people's 'king' (Deut 33:5). The political aspect of the story is the reason why it continues to be so potent today, capable even of interpretations which can be called Marxist (like that of Gottwald), as we shall see in due course.

Settlement in Canaan

The exclusive relationship between Yahweh and Israel was always destined to bring problems. The idea of a people worshipping one god was quite radical in the ancient world, especially as he insisted on forbidding images of himself or anything else (Exod 20:3-5). And it was from the beginning too much for the average Israelite to cope with. This resulted in the famous incident of the making of the Golden Calf (Exod 32), even while the covenant was still being made, and a little later the idolatry with the gods of Moab at the place called Peor (Num 25). The biblical narrative shows in this way that the course of the love affair between Israel and Yahweh will not run smooth.

The point emerges from the next stage in the story, the settlement of Israel in Canaan. The idea of a promised land has loomed large in the story since Genesis 12:1-3, and has been developed in Exodus (Exod 3:17). And the 'conquest' of it is well known from the story of the taking of Jericho, with the walls falling down as the army of Israel marches noisily round them. Exactly how Israel came to be in the land, however, needs careful examination.

The biblical story of the conquest is told in the Book of Joshua. A superficial reading of that book gives the impression that the whole thing was accomplished rather quickly, in the lifetime of Joshua himself (Josh 11:23; 21:45). On more careful inspection, however, it is clear that this was not the case, but rather that the settlement in Canaan was long, difficult and painful (Josh 13:1; 15:63; 17:12-13; Jdg. 1). These passages convey an impression that Israel moved gradually into the land, and had to share it with the already existing population; indeed they were unable to shift that population from certain parts of the land. The whole picture presented by Joshua and Judges together is a kind of contrast between the ideal and the real. The ideal was a swift conquest, with Israel occupying the whole land, so as to be entirely separate from the other nations and their dangerous religious beliefs (Deut 7:1-5). The reality in the narratives corresponds to the actual historical circumstances, in which Israel struggled to gain a foothold in the land at all, and was in fact frequently allured by the temptations of Canaanite religion.

There are a number of modern theories about the history of Israel's arrival in Canaan, some corresponding more than others to the biblical picture. One influential view (that of M. Noth) holds that, while one group of people had an experience of 'exodus' from Egypt, the majority was composed of groups that arrived in a haphazard way from elsewhere. The creation or concept of 'Israel', then, arose only after the arrival of the various peoples who would make it up. It was effected because the exodus group somehow managed to bring others under its umbrella, that is, faith in the God of deliverance as they had experienced him in the desert. Another view is that 'Israel' arose from within the Canaanite population, as a kind of political protest against the oppressive despotism of the Canaanite kingdoms. And a further theory has something of both of these, seeing Israel as composed originally of 'refugees' from political oppression in other parts of the Near East.

One motif that occurs in the discussions is that of the so-called Hapiru, a socially disadvantaged group that is known from the Amarna letters (fourteenth century BCE), and which evidently caused difficulties for some of the Canaanite kings. The term is semantically close to the word 'Hebrew', and this led some to find evidence in the Amarna letters for the presence of Israel in Palestine already at that period. The identification is not certain, however. More relevant is the victory stele of Pharaoh Merenptah, erected after a campaign in Palestine, on which he lists peoples which he subdued, including 'Israel'. The date of the stele is 1207 BCE, confirming that Israel (in some shape or form) had well and truly arrived by that time.

Archaeological evidence helps a little, but in the end is tantalizingly ambiguous. Certain cities which Joshua is said to have conquered (Bethel, Hazor, Debir, Lachish) we know to have been destroyed in the thirteenth century. Unfortunately, however, there is no such evidence for a number of other cities which we are also told fell to Joshua. The celebrated case is Jericho, for which there is not even evidence for habitation at the time in question. To argue from lack of evidence can be a kind of argument from silence, and therefore inconclusive. And the difficulties surrounding the interpretation of data at Jericho in particular are immense. The fact that there is no compelling archaeological evidence for Joshua's conquest in the most likely period for it has no doubt contributed to the belief that the biblical account is somewhat stylized, and that the arrival of Israel was actually more untidy. Others (e.g. Bimson), however, have responded to the evidence by looking elsewhere for a date of the conquest, namely the fifteenth century - a view, however, which has as yet found only a minority following.

———————— The 'Judges Period' ————————

The common threads among the theories are the apparently marginalized nature of early Israel, which was only able to occupy the hill-country - as acknowledged in the biblical accounts - and the unifying factor of the one God Yahweh. These are the elements in the earliest history of Israel in the land.

The first phase of Israel's history in the land falls between the settlement and the establishment of a monarchy, that is (according to the dominant working hypothesis) about 1250-1010 BCE. The latter is more definite than the former, being the date when David is thought to have become king of Israel. Our account of the period comes from the Book of Judges. The length of time allowed for it according to the dates just given is shorter than the time that is apparently required by Judges. When one totals the individual periods given there (typically forty years of peace established by a particular judge; Jdg 3:11; 8:28), a figure of around four hundred years results. There are reasons to think, however, that the numbering is schematized. And in any case it is not clear that the judges whose lives are described in the book lived and worked in strict succession to each other, or that their work actually extended to the whole people and land.

The important historical question concerning this phase of the history is that of the nature and organization of Israel. We have already discussed this in our treatment of ancient Israel as a society (Chapter 1), and will not repeat what was said there. It is important perhaps simply to stress again the concept of the unity of the people at the highest level, that is unity among the tribes. It was here that the concept of 'Israel' would be tested. If the political structure of the nation was rather loose, there was still the crucially important religious sphere in which unity might be expressed.

The focus of unity in this respect was the ark of the covenant. The ark seems to have been stationed in different places at different times - including at least Bethel (Jdg 20:26-27) and Shiloh (1 Sam 3:3). Shiloh seems to have been the recognized centre of Israel's worship for some time (Josh 22; 1 Sam 1-3; Jer 7:12). Furthermore, when David unites north and south in Jerusalem, the ark plays a huge symbolic role in establishing that previously Canaanite city as the centre and capital of all Israel. The ark is the visible link between Israel in Canaan and its origins in the covenant at Sinai. It represents Yahweh's presence with his people, and evidently was thought to have special significance when Israel fought its enemies (1 Sam 4:3). In scholarly discussion the ark has been thought to be the key to the cohesion of Israel in the time of the judges. Noth proposed the special theory that Israel was an 'amphictyony', a term and concept borrowed from a type of tribal organization in ancient Greece, in which member tribes shared a central sanctuary and, in turn, the care of it. That theory, once popular, has been largely rejected now. Yet it remains likely that the ark was the outstanding symbol of the unity of Israel in its early days.

However, the idea of a united people based on a loose tribal structure had strains and stresses built into it. The system was undergirded by the belief that Yahweh himself was 'king'. For this reason Gideon refused an offer of kingship made by the Israelites (Jdg 8:23). It followed too that political institutions were necessarily weak and informally structured. To the average Israelite all this could feel precarious, especially in time of threat from outside. In such circumstances the idea of having a king and a strong army had a real appeal. The dependence on 'charismatic' judges (the term really means 'deliverers'), which was part of the 'Yahweh' package, required a good deal of faith. And it is clear from the accounts of early Israel that implicit faith in Yahweh could not be counted on in Israel. If people wanted a king it might imply that they were in any case more than a little tempted by the gods of Canaan.

Added to this problem is the tendency towards disunity in Israel. There seems to have been a tension in ancient Israel between loyalty to the tribe and loyalty to the whole people. We have seen a glimmer of this in the Song of Deborah (Jdg 5), where certain tribes are blamed for not turning up for the war with Hazor. The point is echoed in other stories too. The tribes that settled east of the Jordan, for example, seem to have felt some isolation from the rest of Israel, and were tempted to establish their own religious life (Josh 22). On another occasion, the tribe of Benjamin found itself at odds with its fellows (Jdg 20). By David's time, there is evidence that internal divisions had settled into a kind of north-south divide, with Judah ranged against the rest (2 Sam 20:1-2). To stresses of this sort were added corruption in the institutions of Israel - in the priesthood (1 Sam 2:12-17), and even in the household of Samuel, the greatest of the judges. For our sources strongly suggest that he had an Achilles' heel, a desire to promote his own family - as unworthy as the sons of Eli - in an institution which was supposed to be charismatic, not dynastic (1 Sam 8:1-3). The combination of these circumstances led to the point where the longing for a king - harboured at least since the time of Gideon (Jdg 8:22) - finally became overwhelming (1 Sam 8:4-5).

———————— Saul and David ————————

The result of the demand for a king was the accession of Saul. This was a dramatic new phase in the history of the people, for from the standpoint of the old traditions it was a rejection of the kingship of Yahweh (1 Sam 8:7). For this reason it was not without opposition, expressed most forcefully by Samuel himself (1 Sam 12:13-25), and even if we do discern the flavour of sour grapes here, it is interesting that the people are finally persuaded that he is right (v.19). It is important for the developing story, however, that Yahweh accedes to the request, misguided though it is, and that once he has done so there is no going back. The issue is a good illustration of the way in which the Bible depicts him as acting with Israel and in their history. There is no coercion here; Israel is called to act responsibly, and must take the consequences of its actions.

The establishment of the kingship is one of the most important events in the history of Israel. It changes things irrevocably, and gives to the Old Testament some of its most enduring language and ideas, including in the end that of the Messiah. The Books of Samuel go to some lengths to justify David's establishment on the throne. While Saul failed because he did not listen to God (1 Sam 13:13), David is presented as one whom God knows inwardly and approves (1 Sam 13:14; 16:7). In the story of rivalry between the two men in 1 Samuel, and the war between the followers of Saul and those of David after the first king's death (2 Sam 2-4), suspicion could easily arise that David had somehow plotted against him. Why, after all, had Jonathan not succeeded his father? David is carefully exonerated from blame in this connection. The friendship between David and Jonathan is part of the picture that is built up of an innocent David who has not sought the throne for himself. He becomes king legitimately, and according to God's purpose.

In the conflict with the house of Saul, however, the delicate politics of the day are made clear. Behind the overt issue of God's preference of one human being over another lies the Realpolitik of internal tensions in Israel. The rivalry between Saul and David corresponds to the division between north and south that we have already noticed (2 Sam 20:1-2). David could first rule only from Hebron, deep in his heartland of Judah, and only afterwards in Jerusalem, when the war against Saul's faction had been resolved (2 Sam 5:5).

In this context the choice of Jerusalem is an act of great political subtlety. It was not an obvious candidate, when compared with places which had been important in Israel's history hitherto, such as Shechem, Bethel or Shiloh. Indeed it was only now possessed by Israel for the first time (2 Sam 5:6-10), because under David the Israelites enjoyed their most sweeping victories since they arrived in Palestine. The mission of Joshua was finally realized. And David capitalized on his gains. The very fact that Jerusalem had not belonged to either side in the war was in its favour; and geographically it lay on the line between north and south, on the borders of Judah and Benjamin. The choice of Jerusalem was a move that could pull together a nation that had a proven tendency to pull apart.

The move had also a strong theological character, of course. In religious terms, David establishes Jerusalem by bearing the ark of the covenant there amid great pomp and ceremony (2 Sam 6; 1 Chr 16). This has the effect of showing that the new place of worship is in a line of succession from the ancient holy places of Israel. Our narrative in 2 Samuel makes explicit that David's selection of Jerusalem is a fulfilment of an ancient promise (2 Sam 7:1, cf. Deut 12:8-11). In the wider Samuel narrative, the triumphal arrival of David in Jerusalem as king is the next stage in the story which began inauspiciously with Saul. Here however the kingship appears as a positive thing. Indeed David is now confirmed in his position with a special promise from Yahweh, delivered by the prophet Nathan, which assures him that, unlike Saul, his son will succeed him on the throne of all Israel, and further, that he will be the father of an everlasting dynasty (2 Sam 7:8-17). This is the so-called Davidic covenant. (The word 'covenant' is not actually used here, but is found in other celebrations of this event, such as 2 Sam 23:5; Ps 89:3).

The new development is a long way from the old idea that Yahweh alone was Israel's king. It is not surprising, therefore, that our texts betray a rather long struggle in reaching this point, a struggle that is essentially about ideas. Not only do we sense hesitation about the institution of kingship in the narrative (1 Sam 8 - 12), but also about the idea of a temple. David's offer to build a temple for Yahweh upon his occupation of Jerusalem is natural enough in the idiom of the ancient Near East, but is first repudiated by Yahweh as alien to his character (2 Sam 7:1-7). Yet both these institutions (king and temple) gain divine acceptance in the end.

More than that, they now become central to the religion of Israel. This is most striking in the Psalms, the hymn-book of the temple, where Jerusalem is celebrated as 'Zion', the holy mountain which Yahweh has chosen for his dwelling-place. The choice of the king and the choice of Zion go closely together, forming the core of what is known as the Zion tradition, or Zion-theology. The classic text is Ps. 2. Here Yahweh declares:

I have set my king on Zion, my holy hill (Ps. 2:6)

The context is a warlike one, in which the Psalmist affirms that Yahweh and his king shall have victory over their enemies. These themes together may be picked up in a number of the 'Zion' Psalms (46; 48; 76; 132). Yahweh dwells on Zion, and this is connected with blessing, peace and protection for his people. But the picture is not complete, for Yahweh, even more remarkably, goes on:

You are my son, today I have begotten you (v. 7).

The unexpectedness of this language lies in the fact that the Old Testament in general does not give a picture of divine kingship in the sense in which we have seen it either in Mesopotamia or in Egypt. (In the latter place, the idea of the king as 'son' of Re' goes back to the third millennium, and is used in the context of the king as an emanation of the sun). Old Testament kings, in contrast, are mere humans, with all the human frailties.

Nevertheless, ideas are borrowed here which have unmistakable echoes of the religion of Canaan. Sometimes this comes across very strongly. For example, in one Psalm we read:

> There is a river whose streams make glad the city of God, the holy habitation of the Most High (Ps 46:4).

In strict geography there is no such thing, merely a stream, the Kidron, which runs quietly past the city in a deep valley on its eastern side, and provides its water. Here there is a distant echo of the Canaanite idea that the gods dwell at the source of all the waters (an idea which we also found echoed in Gen 2:10-14). Nor are we in the realm of geography when Jerusalem is located in the 'far north' (Ps. 48:1). This too arises from Canaan in the location of the temple of Baal to the north of Palestine. His mountain is Mount Zaphon, which literally means 'north'. The psalmody of Israel, indeed, sometimes sees Zion as the true mountain of God as opposed to Zaphon, its pale rival (Ps 68:15-16). This is one effect of the figurative borrowing of Canaanite language.

What do we make of these cadences of Canaan, in view of what we have seen of the programme which we find in parts of the Old Testament story to oppose and root out the Canaanite religion in all its forms? On one view, it all arose from David's choice of Jerusalem as his capital. Jerusalem was essentially a Canaanite city. We met it first, it will be recalled, in the story of Abraham, when the patriarch was met at 'Salem' by Melchizedek, the priest-king of the city. There was, then, already an ancient religious tradition at the site. Furthermore, there was a hint in that same story of the possibility of somehow taking over the worship of El, specifically El Elyon, into the worship of Yahweh (Gen 14:18-22). How far was David aiming to suggest that El Elyon of Jebus was none other than Yahweh of Israel when he bore the ark of the covenant to the city amid great pomp and ceremony (2 Sam 6; 1 Chr 16)? Did he locate the ark at the site of the sanctuary of El Elyon, and is that where Solomon would in due course build the temple? The latter location is identified by a special angelic revelation (2 Sam 24), and we do not know whether this was a new temple site or the old Canaanite one.

Some hold that David actually intended to establish continuity with the Canaanite religion, in order to try to unite a population which was by no means purely Israelite. His new high priest Zadok is even held to have strong Canaanite associations; the name (which means 'righteous') is very close to part of the name

Melchizedek ('my king is righteousness'), and this may be related to vocabulary used in worship in Jebus.

If this view is correct, it means that David's political stratagem in selecting Jerusalem was even more cunning than a plan merely to unite the northern and southern parts of his new kingdom. We cannot be sure how far David actively assimilated elements of the Canaanite religion into his new order of things. Nevertheless, the sudden rise of Jerusalem to prominence in the history of Israel was to change its character irrevocably, and affect its further development profoundly.

——— 'Solomon in all his Glory' ———

After the victory, the peace, reflected even in the name of Solomon (akin to Shalom). And with this son of David comes the greatest splendour of Israel. Solomon is remembered as the king who asked for wisdom not wealth, and was given both in large measure (1 Kgs 3). He surpassed the wisdom of the east (1 Kgs 4:29-34), and his riches were worth the Queen of Sheba's long journey from the southern deserts to see (1 Kgs 9). 'The king made silver as common in Jerusalem as stones, and he made cedars as numerous as the sycamores of the Shephelah' (1 Kgs 10:27).

When Solomon succeeded David in c. 970 BCE the great powers of the ancient world were at a low ebb. It was a lull between the hegemony of Egypt's New Kingdom and the tidal wave of Assyria that would soon engulf the region. And in that moment of history, modest Israel could don imperial robes. Solomon controlled an area from the border with Egypt in the southern Negeb to Hamath in the far north, thus holding sway in that perpetually disputed arena. He refortified many cities (Megiddo, Hazor, Lachish, Gezer, Beth-Shemesh). He laid weaker nations under tribute. And as we have seen already in our discussion of trade in the region, he grew rich on the traffic that must pass through his land. There was peace, prosperity and perhaps a flowering of culture, if the king's reputation for wisdom is evidence of such.

The capstone of his reign, of course, was the building of the temple, the narrative of which occupies four chapters (1 Kgs 5-8) of the story of his life. This, together with the completion of his palace and the acquisition of a huge harem, made him a proper oriental potentate. Perhaps it was a case of pride leading to a fall, for from these dizzy heights, the kingdom was to fall sharply into weakness and division. The account in Kings knows of a decisive turning-point in Solomon's life from loyalty to Yahweh to the pursuit of other gods, and the end of the story is one of rampant apostasy. The theological account matches this to a loss of power, and inroads into the king's sphere of authority by subject rulers (1 Kgs 11).

The crucial upshot of this fall from grace was the division of the kingdom. The death of Solomon apparently allowed the release of pent-up frustrations in the populace, many of whom undoubtedly suffered at the hands of their ambitious overlord. The new king Rehoboam could not match his father's authority, with the result that the largest part of the kingdom threw off the yoke of Jerusalem, and set up its own rival kingdom under the one-time servant Jeroboam. The success of Jeroboam in gaining widespread support represents a reassertion of the old tendency to inner division within the nation. In reality, perhaps, it was only the unusual leadership qualities of David, and the massive administrative success of Solomon that could suppress the tendency to divide. It is very telling that Jeroboam's appeal to the people of Israel looks like a reaction against the old upstart from the deep south, and a call to return to the old ways of tribal independence (1 Kgs 12:16).

Nevertheless, Jeroboam too becomes a king, and mimics the royal paraphernalia of Judah and Jerusalem by setting up his own state sanctuaries in Bethel and Dan. Here too he appeals to old traditions, especially at Bethel, because of its associations with the patriarchs. The cult at Bethel effectively becomes his official state religion, just like the cult at Jerusalem in the south. Indeed it is consciously intended to replace it, for he knows the power of great sanctuaries in people's minds (1 Kgs 12:27).

Jeroboam's most memorable contribution to history is his 'golden calves', so reminiscent of the ancient folly at Sinai (Exod 32). Why did he embrace a policy apparently so much at odds with the ancient imageless religion? It is sometimes said that the calves were not intended to be images of gods at all, but merely pedestals of the invisible god; contemporary Canaanite iconography is cited in support, there being some cases of calf or bull figures bearing the images of gods. However, the weight of the evidence is on the other side, and it is likely that Jeroboam did intend to make images. There might have been political astuteness in this, a piece of one-upmanship in the propaganda war with Jerusalem which could boast no image. It should be borne in mind that Israelite religion was in practice of mixed character; Solomon himself had made images, and their appeal in the popular mind was no doubt powerful. The interesting question is whether Jeroboam intended his images as representations of Yahweh or another deity. The connection with Yahweh is suggested by his claim that these 'gods' had brought the people out of Egypt (1 Kgs 12:28). The bull symbolism, on the other hand, may be suggestive of El. Jeroboam's official religion, therefore, probably involved a syncretism (that is, a religious mix) of Yahweh and El. But whereas in Jerusalem El was somehow assimilated to Yahweh, in Jeroboam's kingdom Yahweh is rather built into El.

In any case with Jeroboam there is a new star in the constellation of ancient states. For the next stage of Israel's history we must speak of two kingdoms, the northern, often known simply as 'Israel' in our texts, and the southern, or Judah. After 1 Kings 12, the remainder of the books of Kings is taken up with their story. It is a story in which politics and religion are closely linked.

— The Kingdoms of Israel and Judah —
to the Exile

The history of Israel has by now moved a long way, from the tribal league with no central institutions and Yahweh as 'king', to a pair of minor kingdoms, each with its own temple-palace institutions, looking somewhat similar to the Canaanite states that had preceded them. As such they enter the normal political flux of their times, in a scenario of wars, and intermittently of relative peace and prosperity. Israel and Syria were often at war (1 Kgs 20), as were the two kingdoms themselves (1 Kgs 15:32), though they could on other occasions make common cause (1 Kgs 22; 2 Kgs 3). Rehoboam, Solomon's successor in Jerusalem, quickly felt his weakness when invaded by Pharaoh Sheshonq 1 (1 Kgs 14:25-28, where he is called Shishak). The northern kingdom fared better initially, and enjoyed periods of relative power. King Omri, the less well known father of the infamous Ahab, founded the only real dynasty that the northern kingdom would know, and made his capital at Samaria. His relative power in the early ninth century BCE is attested by the famous Moabite Stone, an inscription by Mesha, king of Moab, in which he records Omri's subjugation of his nation. Mesha, however, also records certain successes against Israel, so the ninth century seems to have been one of mixed fortunes. The following century brought long spells of peace and prosperity to both kingdoms, under Azariah (Uzziah) in Judah (791-740 BCE), and Jeroboam II in the north (793-753 BCE). The latter was able to retake tracts of territory earlier lost to Syria, because of the weakness of that nation.

The calm was soon shattered, however, with the rise of the sleeping giant Assyria. In the latter half of the eighth century, Tiglath-Pileser III began conquests in the region which would lead to Assyrian dominance in Palestine and beyond, into Egypt itself, for the next century or more. Samaria fell to Shalmaneser V in 722 BCE, and its people went into exile in parts of the Assyrian empire, for ever lost to history. (The myth of the 'lost tribes of Israel' arises from this event.) Judah escaped the fate of its northern neighbour at that time. Twenty years later (701 BCE), however, another Assyrian king, Sennacherib, ravaged the cities of Judah. Among the devastations wrought then, the fate of Lachish, a southern border town of Judah, stands out. Reliefs of the siege, made after the event by the conqueror to decorate the walls of his palace at Nineveh, and now in the British Museum, depict the stages of the siege: the siegeworks, the resistance from the walls, the capture of the city, the exemplary flaying alive of leaders of the city, and the sad procession into exile. It is an eloquent picture of the famed ruthless cruelty of the Assyrian.

Only Jerusalem held out. We have two historical accounts of this, one from the Bible and the other from Assyria! The Old Testament's view of the event occurs twice, in 2 Kings 18-19 and Isaiah 36-37. It records the brash boasting of the Assyrian commander, who brags that no god has been able to stand against the gods of Assyria (2 Kgs 18:34-35). The story ends with the miraculous deliverance of the city against all odds and expectations (2 Kgs 19:35-37). The Assyrian memory of the incident comes from King Sennacherib's own account of his Palestinian campaign. In the arrogant style of such accounts he boasts of how he has laid waste Judah, but of Jerusalem he only says the he 'shut up Hezekiah like a bird in a cage'.

Had Sennacherib taken Jerusalem he would certainly have made the most of it in his campaign write-up. So the report is significant for what it does not say, and is a confirmation that indeed he was unable to take Jerusalem. Not surprisingly, he says nothing about the phenomenal devastation of his army recorded in the Bible. But it is clear that Jerusalem survived - and its survival at this point may have been extremely significant, for it allowed Judah to continue as a nation. However, it was henceforth no more than a vassal state, and when

Assyria fell in 612 BCE to the new power in the area, Babylon, the writing was on the wall for Judah too.

The events thus briefly described show something of the dilemmas of the kings of Israel and Judah. Their kingdoms were born in relative strength, but they were often weak. Though a Jeroboam II might be a minor power in the immediate neighbourhood of Israel, the underlying tendency in the politics of the region was for imperial power to increase. And therefore no sensible estimate of the chances of the two kingdoms could have been optimistic about their survival. To the kings, in these circumstances, it could seem that security lay in their relations with the great powers. There were, of course, no guaranteed favours from the mighty. The tricky situation of King Ahaz is a case in point.

Ahaz reigned in Judah in c. 735-716. In his time, he was threatened by an alliance of Israel (the northern kingdom) and Syria, further to the north. To protect himself he appealed to Assyria, and when the Assyrians marched into Damascus, killing the Syrian king (2 Kgs 16:9), Ahaz seemed to have backed the right horse. The price, however, was religious capitulation, for we are told that he deliberately remodelled worship in the Jerusalem temple in the Assyrian style; and he did it 'because of the king of Assyria' (2 Kgs 16:10-16). From this time Judah was effectively a vassal of Assyria, and the covenant with Yahweh was severely compromised, at least in the official state religion.

In similar vein, Hoshea, the last king of Israel (732-722), decided to try to throw off Assyrian overlordship by turning to Egypt - the only possible alternative. Whatever his reading of the times, he got it wrong and took the consequences (2 Kgs 17).

With Israel fallen, the final stage of Judah's history is also a story of dangerous relations with the neighbouring powers. Hezekiah tried to turn back to Yahweh, and is commended in the biblical account for his faith. But he obviously had limited success, and was forced to pay tribute, and his kingdom suffered dreadfully in the process. His successor Manasseh ruled for a large part of the seventh century, and knuckled down to Assyria. With Josiah, however, one of the most important moments in Judah's history occurred, which would not stem the tide of imperial aggression, but which nevertheless would have a lasting effect on the life of God's people.

When Josiah became king in about 640 BCE, Assyrian power was on the wane, and Babylon had not yet filled the vacuum. In 628 he undertook a reform of religion in Judah, which involved desecrating places of worship up and down the country, and centring the official religion on Jerusalem, which he purified from the accoutrements of foreign religion (2 Kgs 22-23). This was, of course, not merely a religious act, because as we have seen, religion was inseparable from politics. In turning Judah back to Yahweh, he was declaring independence from Assyria. Our accounts even tell us that he marched into the territory of the former northern kingdom and desecrated places of false worship there.

Josiah's reform, as it is called, obviously struck a chord with many in Judah. The Assyrianizing of the kings had not necessarily reflected the religious colour of the whole population. That was no doubt very mixed. But it seems that in Josiah's day there was what might be called a reform party, that is, those who wanted to re-establish the ancient Yahwistic religion of Israel. The power base of this movement may have been in parts of the countryside, among conservative people who harked back to the old tribal ways. But it appears to have included very influential people too.

Josiah died in 609 BCE, vainly trying to prevent Pharaoh Neco from passing through Israelite territory, as the pharaoh marched against the advance of Babylon. This was a terrible blow to the cause of independence, and apparently to the worship of Yahweh. Josiah's successors were forced to try to come to terms with the imperial powers. The issue again in Palestine was whether it would be dominated by the new Mesopotamian power, Babylon, or whether Egypt would prevail, and the kings of Judah looked first one way then the other (2 Kgs 23:33-24:1). Because of King Jehoiakim's Egyptian sympathies, Judah fell under suspicion in his reign, and the Babylonians, under King Nebuchadrezzar, took action against him (2 Kgs 24:2). Then soon after the accession of his son Jehoiachin (597 BCE), they took the opportunity of putting in their own puppet, Zedekiah, at the same time taking off the first wave of captives to their own land (2 Kgs 24:10-17)

The last stage in Judah's story concerns a feeble attempt to reinstate the independence policy of Josiah. The 'reform party' exercised a strong influence over Zedekiah, who was accordingly unable to heed the message of the prophet Jeremiah. That message, briefly, warned that Zedekiah should surrender, because Yahweh had determined to hand the people over to Babylon as a punishment for the nation's sins. The king may have wanted to listen, but he was afraid to be seen openly conversing with the prophet, for fear of his hawkish officials (Jer 38:24-28). In the biblical account, however, it was now too late for reform and independence, and the refusal to heed Jeremiah had disastrous results. The Babylonians came again in 587, destroyed the temple, and put an end to the kingdom of Judah for ever (2 Kgs 25).

It is an ironic end to the story of the nation that had begun so hopefully with an escape from the grip of an empire, that it should go back to its former condition of enslavement. The analogy between Egypt of old and the new captivity in Babylon is not lost on the biblical writers. The possibility of such an exile is envisaged in the so-called 'curses of the covenant' in Deuteronomy (Deut 28:68, where 'Egypt' may be taken as a reference to any nation that makes Israel captive). The new enslavement, therefore, was the work of the same God who had once delivered them! The journey of the people of Yahweh had somehow gone badly wrong.

——— Religion under the Kings ———

The end of the two kingdoms was not the end of the story, nor even of the people of Yahweh. The story is rather one of adaptation to the new conditions, as we shall see in a moment.

Before looking at the exile, however, we must notice briefly some important reactions to the religious policies of the kings. The main religious development in the period was the rise of the prophetic movement. This reached its height in the eighth century BCE, with Amos, Hosea, Isaiah and Micah, though the phenomenon had earlier origins. A fuller account of the prophets and their message must await the next chapter. It is enough to observe at this point that the policies of the kings did not go unchallenged in either Israel or Judah. The religious situation was a mixed one. There were always those, it seems, who remained faithful to Yahweh, even though the pressures to fall in with the prevailing Baalism must have been enormous. When the prophet Elijah, in Ahab's reign in the ninth century, complained in despair that he was the only one left who was faithful, Yahweh himself told him firmly that he was not (1 Kgs 19:14, 18). Elijah and his successors emerged from the ranks of these conservative Israelites. Very broadly, the prophets challenged the kings to turn back to the ancient ways; or to put it differently, to be faithful to the covenant. (We shall have to look more carefully at this idea in the next chapter.)

Besides the prophetic movement, another tendency should be observed, namely what we have already called the reform movement. This was not identical with the prophetic movement. We observe it in the tendency towards reform of the worship from time to time, at least in Judah, as reported in the Books of Kings. Josiah was not the first, therefore, to set such a reform in train. Reforms went back to Asa in the early ninth century, and included that of Hezekiah, the most far-reaching prior to Josiah (2 Kgs 18:1-8). The reform movement, then, may have had much earlier origins than Josiah, based on certain officials and local leaders up and down the land. In biblical scholarship, this movement is widely associated with the Book of Deuteronomy, which is generally held to have been composed in the seventh century. We shall return to this issue also in due course.

How this reform movement related to the prophets is not clear. But there were obviously features in common between them. The Book of Hosea, most noticeably, has similarities of thought and language with Deuteronomy. The Books of Kings too, which are regarded as 'deuteronomic', and may themselves come out of the reform party, have a high regard for the prophets (2 Kgs 17). It is clear, then, that Josiah's reform did not come out of nothing. There must have been some measure of real support in the country for it. Unfortunately, however, it did not seem to represent the dominant tone of the national life over the centuries. And it could not turn back what the Old Testament presents as God's judgment on Israel and Judah, by means of political realities, for their chronic unfaithfulness to the ancient covenant.

The Exile

In 587 BCE the very heart of the belief system of Judah was torn out. If a Judahite had been asked, in the time of Josiah, what were the main pillars of his or her faith (or of the covenant), he or she would have identified three things: the king, the temple and the land. It is a combination that had, by then, ancient credentials. The land had been promised in the mists of antiquity to Abraham, and taken in due course by Joshua. Temple and king had been in place since the hey-day of the united nation, and life in the seventh century was unthinkable without them. It was to preserve these that kings had acted as they had done, according to their lights. For the Judahite, these three things quite simply represented the substance of the people's relationship with Yahweh. It could be called their world-view. While the temple was in place, and the king on his throne, all was well; God was pleased with his people.

But now these three pillars had fallen. The Davidic dynasty was brought once and for all to an end. The temple lay in ruins. And the majority, or at least the élite, of the people had been removed by force from their land. It is hard to think of a greater trauma for a people. In 587 BCE begins what we know as the 'exile'. It is a relatively short period, which may be counted from 587 to 539 BCE, when some of the exiles began to return to the land. But besides being painful, it was one of the most dynamic and productive spells in the life of the people. From this point, incidentally, Judahites may now be called Jews, a term which betokens the change in their status – no longer a nation with a king and cult-centre like other nations, but a community that must find its identity in other ways.

They were not entirely bereft of help from the past. A further element in their faith, which may well be regarded as a fourth 'pillar', was, to use a broad term, the Word of Yahweh. Again, we leave aside for now the account of the formation of what we know as the books of the Old Testament. But whether in the form of laws, prophetic sayings, wisdom sayings, narratives or songs (the Psalms), a rich tradition had been building up. It is likely that the experience of exile gave impetus to the growth of the idea of 'scripture'. The sayings of prophets, for example, may now have been gathered into collections. And though we cannot be certain, it is possible that the institution of the synagogue had its origins in these times, to foster the habit of reading and meditating on the scriptures. A number of books, and parts of books, were also written in this period, including the Books of Kings for example, and the Book of Lamentations.

Restoration

The tide turned in 539 BCE. The immediate cause was a change, once again, of imperial overlord. The Babylonian empire declined rapidly after the death of Nebuchadnezzar in 562 BCE. In that year his successor Amel-Marduk (or Evil-Merodach, as he is known in the Old Testament) released King Jehoiachin from prison (2 Kgs 25:27-30). This might have been a straw in the wind, suggesting that better times were coming. But the decisive change came because of the weakness of the last king of Babylon, Nabonidus (556-539 BCE), who abandoned the capital for the Arabian desert. It is not clear why he did this; it may have had something to do with his personal allegiance to the god Sin, rather than Marduk. In any case, his departure left the way open for revolution in Babylon itself. It came in the form of a bloodless coup, carried out by Cyrus, a Median, whose restoration of the neglected worship of Marduk was welcome and popular.

Cyrus's restoration of Marduk was an example of a general policy. This is expressed in his own words in the so-called 'Cyrus Cylinder', a cylinder of baked clay, now kept in the British Museum, which bears the inscription: 'I returned to their places [the gods who had been brought to Babylon] and housed them in lasting abodes. I gathered together all their inhabitants and restored [to them] their dwellings'. The Jews were obviously among those who benefited. Indeed, a specific charter for their return, from Cyrus himself, is recorded in Ezra 1:2-4. This is more than just permission; Cyrus claims to have received a charge from none other than Yahweh to rebuild his house in Jerusalem.

The return home (for those who went) began in 537 BCE, and continued gradually over the decades that followed. Indeed, when Ezra the scribe went back to Judah almost a century later (in 458 BCE) he took a fresh group of immigrants with him (Ezra 7:6-7). Among the first leaders of the community, however, was Zerubbabel, a grandson of King Jehoiachin (Ezra 3:2; Matt 1:12) – despite his Babylonian name (apparently meaning 'seed of Babylon')! He seems briefly to have been the focus of Messianic hopes for the restoration of the Davidic monarchy, though this did not happen. The first steps towards reconstituting the community in Judah were religious, and Zerubbabel, together with the priest Jeshua (or Joshua), laid the foundation of the new temple (Ezra 3). The building was completed in 516 BCE, after setbacks due to local opposition (Ezra 4), but spurred on finally by the prophecies of Haggai and Zechariah (Ezra 5:1-2; 6:15). This opposition to the community's presence, in a curiously modern echo, continued during the next century, as the non-chronological report in Ezra 4 makes clear, with its pattern of appeals from local administrators to the imperial overlords against Jerusalem's consolidation (4:5-7).

It was in the middle of this next century, however, that the community took decisive steps forward. The two great figures of this time were Ezra and Nehemiah. The traditional understanding of their ministries is that Ezra arrived first, in 458 BCE, and Nehemiah later, in 444 BCE, but that there was a time when they were present and active together, as supposed in Nehemiah 8. The actual chronology is one of the conundrums of Old Testament study (and a favourite essay topic for students!) and according to one view, it was Nehemiah who came first, with Ezra following, possibly in 398 BCE. The specific reasons for this have to be pursued in the commentaries. In the present state of enquiry, opinions on the matter are finely balanced, but there is some resurgence of the traditional view.

We can be more sure of their respective purposes in coming to Jerusalem. Ezra's was strictly religious. He was 'a scribe, skilled in the law of Moses that the LORD the God of Israel had given', and he had the blessing of the imperial authorities for his mission (Ezra 7:6). He found Judah in a state of religious disorder, the chief cause being a habit of intermarriage with non-Jewish neighbours. Ezra's response was scarcely ecumenical! He saw extreme danger to Judaism, and took severe measures to purify the community (Ezra 9-10).

Nehemiah was driven by the need to rebuild the city's fortifications. There may have been an earlier attempt to rebuild these at some time after the return from Babylon, and they may have been reduced once more as part of the successful action of local enemies against the new community. Nehemiah now receives official sanction for the project of rebuilding, and this time – again in the teeth of opposition (Neh 4-6) – the plan succeeds (6:15).

————— To the End of ————— the Old Testament Period

The stage was now set for the final act in the history of the Old Testament period. Jerusalem was established as the city of the Jews, and Jews settled too in neighbouring towns in Judah. They were a people united by their religion. The city may have had walls, but these spoke only of imperial tolerance, not of real political strength. The heart of the community was the temple worship, and the other aspects of religious life, especially the growing place of scripture. What we know as the Old Testament 'canon' probably began to be formed in these times, as we shall see a little later. Traditionally, it was Ezra who gave the impetus to this religious development. Already in his time, we see the beginnings of the interpretation of scripture which would be such an important factor in Judaism (Neh 8:1-8). Little more is known of the community between Ezra and Nehemiah in the fifth century and the second century BCE. The prophet Malachi worked in the period, with his picture of general decline in religion, and perhaps of material poverty. The Books of Chronicles are dated variously from 400-200 BCE, and their message of encouragement gives evidence of hopes for the restoration of the Davidic monarchy. The Samaritan sect probably came into existence about the time of Alexander, following some breach with the religious authorities in Jerusalem. They built a temple on Mt. Gerizim, near ancient Shechem, and began to interpret the old traditions as if they themselves were the true inheritors of the covenantal promises to Israel. They produced their own version of the Torah (see further Chapter 3 on the composition of the Old Testament).

Generally, the history of the period is now a story of successive empires in the area. Persian rule collapsed before the advance of Alexander the Great in 331 BCE, and his Greek, or Hellenistic, empire – though it soon fragmented – lasted until 63 BCE. It was in turn replaced by the rising Roman power, which would supply the political background to the New Testament, as well as to the rabbinic age. Judaism developed in this context, a religious community in a world of empire, more or less benignly tolerated. Some of its literature in the late biblical period derives from this context. The Wisdom of Sirach, or Ecclesiasticus, dates from around 200 BCE, and shows the importance to the Jews then both of the temple and priesthood, and of the Torah. For the former, there is a memorable portrait of the High Priest, Simon II, around 200 BCE, decked out in splendour for his duties at the altar (Sirach 50:1-21). And for the latter, the old idea of 'wisdom' has become equated with Torah. This book is a legacy of traditional pious Judaism in the middle of the so-called Seleucid period (the division of Alexander's empire that controlled Palestine).

It was a few decades after this, however, that a major crisis blew up. The Seleucid King Antiochus IV 'Epiphanes', pressed for funds to sustain military campaigns, plundered the Jerusalem temple. He also re-dedicated it to the god Zeus (1 Maccabees 2:29-38), which was, of course, a desecration of it in the eyes of traditional Jews. Judaism, however, had become mixed in these early decades of the century. Many leading Jews had become aligned with the ruling power, culturally and economically. These are termed 'Hellenizing' Jews, to distinguish them from the traditionalists. Some, for example, became tax-collectors for their political masters, as is familiar to readers of the New Testament. And in the 170sBCE, the high priesthood itself fell to the Hellenizers, with the result that Antiochus IV's first plundering of the temple met little resistance from the religious authorities.

Nevertheless, there was a backlash from traditional Jews. At first their resistance was patient; the origin of the 'Hasidim' belongs in this time. But the outrages of Antiochus so infuriated some that they took up arms. The 'Maccabean' revolt was led by a priest, Mattathiah, and his sons. ('Maccabeus' was a nickname, meaning 'hammerer', and was applied particularly to Mattathiah's son Judas. The family name was 'Hasmon', hence the term 'Hasmonean', by which they are also known.) It began in the town of Modin, in 167 BCE, when Mattathiah killed a Jew who was sacrificing to a pagan god, and also the official who was supervising the sacrifice (1 Maccabees 2:15-28).

This was war, and at first the Maccabean forces were astonishingly successful, due both to the brilliance of Judas and to Seleucid commitments elsewhere. Jewish worship was re-established in 164 BCE, and the temple rid of its pagan trappings and re-dedicated. The Jewish Feast of Hanukkah still celebrates the event. There were reverses, however, and Judas died in battle in 161 BCE. Nevertheless, his brothers Jonathan and Simon, by accommodation with the authorities, held the office of High Priest, and Simon was in addition proclaimed 'ethnarch' by the Jewish people (142 BCE). This was the effective beginning of what is known as the Hasmonean dynasty, its leaders ruling like minor kings with imperial support, though the title of king was taken first by Aristobulus I (104-103 BCE). The latter Hasmoneans enjoyed some military strength. John Hyrcanus (134-104 BCE) defeated the Idumeans to the south, forcing them to become Jews, and expanded into Transjordan. Alexander Janneus (103-76 BCE), a cruel despot, continued his expansionist policy.

The Hasmoneans survived the transition to Roman rule in Palestine in 63 BCE, until its last representative, Antigonus, fell from grace and was executed in 38 BCE. The Romans continued to allow a degree of autonomy, however. And under their protection an Idumean Jew, educated at Rome, and married to a Hasmonean, filled the political vacuum. He would be known to history as Herod the Great (38-4 BCE). But his story belongs more appropriately to an account of the New Testament.

The period just outlined finds echoes in some of the late Old Testament literature. The clearest of these are in the Book of Daniel, which takes a predominantly negative view of the empires from Babylon to Greece, and focuses especially on the outrages of Antiochus IV (as we shall see in the next chapter). The most important legacy of the period, however, is the fragmentation of Judaism arising from different attitudes to the ruling powers. The official Jewish authorities became predominantly (but not exclusively) Hellenist. The Sadducees, a ruling party familiar from the New Testament, formed part of this tendency. Traditional Judaism, on the other hand, was reflected principally in movements such as the Hasidim, and later the Pharisees. The group known as Essenes took a radical view of the corruption of the temple, and withdrew from mainstream religious and social life.

They are best known as the sect that formed the Qumran community on the shores of the Dead Sea, and collected and produced the documents that we call the Dead Sea Scrolls. To this range of Jewish movements may be added the 'Zealots'. These took their inspiration from the Maccabeans, and kept alive the tradition of resistance to imperial rule. When the most effective Jewish revolt of the first century came (66-73 CE), however, it was a more broadly based movement within Judaism.

A final important point must be made about the history of the Jews after the exile, namely that they did not all return to Palestine. Many stayed in Babylon, and others even went further east, to the heart of the Persian empire (see the Book of Esther). Some, of course, had not gone to Babylon in the first place, but to Egypt, as we know from the Book of Jeremiah (Jer 40-44). In a sense, then, the 'exile' did not finally end in 539 BCE.

The form of Judaism that proved most resilient at the time was undoubtedly that which emerged as rabbinic Judaism. This was the successor of the traditional forms of the faith from the Hasidim to the Pharisees, that had their origins in a concern for faithfulness to the old ways. Significantly, it developed in both Babylon and Palestine. That is to say, it was a form of Judaism that did not depend on possessing or dwelling in the ancient promised land. In the debate within Judaism concerning the nature of its relation to political power, the way of resistance and independence lost the argument. Or at least it did so until the present century.

Further Reading

J. Bright,   *A History of Israel*, SCM, London, third edition, 1981

M. Noth,   *The History of Israel*, A. and C. Black, London, 1958

P. R. Davies, *'Ancient Israel'*, JSOT Press, Sheffield, 1992 (repr 1995) (this is a critique of traditional approaches)

R. de Vaux, *Ancient Israel: its Life and Institutions*, DLT, London, 1961

G. W. Ramsey, *The Quest for the Historical Israel*, London, SCM, 1982 (this contains a review of various recent approaches)

R. Albertz, *A History of Israelite Religion in the Old Testament Period* (Volume I), SCM, London, 1994

3

CONTENTS AND COMPOSITION

Introduction

In our surveys of history and geography, we have thought a good deal about what lies behind the Old Testament, and have even referred to it frequently along the way. But it is time now to come to the thing itself, the Old Testament as a book. This is the most obvious as well as the most important thing about it. For the location of the events and their reconstruction through the periods of history are nothing in themselves. It is not just that we would know little of these things without the information in the book; more importantly, it is the existence of the book itself that testifies to one of history's great religious experiences. This then is the subject of the present chapter. What is in the Old Testament, and how did it come into being?

These two questions relate to 'composition' in two slightly different senses. Part of our concern here is simply to say what is in the Old Testament – composition in the sense of the sum of the parts, or components. This leads to an associated question: how was the Old Testament formed? In the present chapter we shall ask the 'contents' question first, and begin to ask questions about formation. This second topic, however, will occupy us also in the next chapter.

It goes without saying that our 'book', the Old Testament, is really not one book but a collection of books, thirty-nine in number. The collection represents a long story of composing and gathering, involving different periods of the history which we have studied, and many different types of literature and even purposes in writing. But is there a basic way into dividing up or classifying this extensive literature?

Our English Old Testaments tell us little, on the surface, about the organization of their subject matter. The Hebrew Old Testament, however (or Hebrew Bible, as it should be called), is more helpful. For it typically describes itself by the simple use of three words on the front cover and spine of the book: Torah, Prophets, Writings. (Jewish readers, indeed, sometimes refer to it as the TANAK, an acronym based on the initial letters of the three words in Hebrew). This is a useful first hint that the books may fall into categories. It is a little complicated by the fact that the division which we find in the Hebrew Bible does not wholly correspond with that of the Christian Bible; yet there is sufficient correspondence to allow us to use the threefold division as a guide.

The Pentateuch

The first division is the first five books of the Bible: Genesis, Exodus, Leviticus, Numbers and Deuteronomy. These are traditionally known as the Five Books of Moses (German Bibles, for example, still use the names 1-5 Moses instead of the names that are more familiar to English readers). These books are also known as the Torah by Jewish readers, and the Pentateuch by Christians (a term based on Greek words for 'five' and 'scroll'). The special names used by both Jews and Christians mark it out as a section that is self-contained and that enjoys a certain primacy, and perhaps special authority, in the life of the believing community.

The Pentateuch is the foundational document of biblical religion. This is so because it tells the story of the beginnings of Israel, the people of God, and as such is a kind of charter for their existence, their life and worship and their occupancy of their land. It begins with the creation of the world and the spread of the nations throughout it (Gen 1-11). It then focuses on one family, that of Abraham, who is chosen by God to become the ancestor of a people, Israel. With this people he will have a special relationship, he will give them a land, and even entrust them with a mission, to bring blessing to all nations (Gen 12-50). It goes on to tell of the establishment of the relationship with Israel (Exodus, Leviticus), and of its early difficulties (Exodus, Numbers), before they enter the promised land and set out on their life with God. In fact, the possession of the land does not take place within the Pentateuch itself, but leaves

The Books of the Old Testament - in the order

Genesis	**Torah**
Exodus	
Leviticus	
Numbers	
Deuteronomy	
Joshua	**The Prophets**
Judges	(Former Prophets)
1 Samuel	
2 Samuel	
1 Kings	
2 Kings	
Isaiah	(Major prpohetic books)
Jeremiah	
Ezekiel	
Hosea	(Minor Prophets: the Book of the Trwlve)
Joel	
Amos	
Obadiah	
Jonah	
Micah	
Nahum	
Habakkuk	
Zephaniah	
Haggai	
Zechariah	
Malachi	

of the Jewish Scriptures

Psalms   The Writings
Job
Proverbs
Ruth
Song of Songs
Ecclesiastes
Lamentations
Esther
Daniel
Ezra
Nehemiah
Chronicles

Their order in Christian Bibles

Genesis
Exodus
Leviticus
Numbers
Deuteronomy
Joshua
Judges
Ruth
1 Samuel
2 Samuel
1 Kings
2 Kings
1 Chronicles
2 Chronicles
Ezra
Nehemiah
Esther
Job
Psalms
Proverbs
Ecclesiastes
Song of Songs
Isaiah
Jeremiah
Lamentations
Ezekiel
Daniel
Hosea
Joel
Amos
Obadiah
Jonah
Micah
Nahum
Habakkuk
Zephaniah
Haggai
Zechariah
Malachi

Moab', and consists largely of exhortations addressed to the people before they enter. (For fuller accounts of the Pentateuch as a 'story', see Clines, Blenkinsopp.) The story, therefore, has great potency as a religious document, for it has enormous scope (a view of the world and all nations), explanatory power (who Israel is) and direction for living.

Let us now look more closely at the contents of the Pentateuch, book by book.

Genesis

Genesis may be divided into two principal parts, the 'primeval history' (Gen 1-11) and the 'patriarchal narratives' (Gen 12-50). The primeval history concerns the origins of humanity. It opens with an account of creation, or as scholars usually hold, two separate creation accounts, now combined (Gen 1:1-2:3 [or 4a], and 2:4 [or 4b]-3:24; see further below on this). The first gives humanity (*'adam*) its place in the world order. In the second, the term *'adam* applies to the first human being, a man who in due course finds a woman to be his counterpart; the second account thus focuses on the relationship between the man and the woman and their place together in their immediate environment. The account includes an explanation of the institution of marriage (2:24-25).

It does not finish there, however, but goes on with the well-known story of the first human disobedience, and its consequences. This was not summary death (as might have been expected from 2:17), but the pronouncement of a 'curse' on the earth (3:17) and a disruption in the relationships which the creation had put together. The ensuing narratives show that death has, after all, become a normal and inevitable feature of the continuing story of humanity (4:8-24; 5).

The creation accounts lead into the flood-narrative (6:5-9:17), the story of a great punishment sent by God because of the ever-increasing wickedness of humanity (6:5-7). The inundation of the earth is a kind of return to the first formlessness out of which God had shaped the ordered world (1:2). It proves not to be the final act in the drama of human history, because of God's decision to spare Noah and his family. There is, therefore, a new beginning after the flood, with Noah cast as a new Adam, and many echoes between the story of new beginnings and that of first beginnings (9:1-7).

Finally, the nations spread out over the earth (Gen 10), in a kind of fulfilment of the first command to humanity (1:28; 9:1), with only a cloud cast by the act of pride in the building of the Tower of Babel, in fulfilment of the first command to humanity (1:28; 9:1), with only a cloud cast by the act of pride in the building of the Tower of Babel, in the light of which the spread of the peoples can be seen as a punishment and a disintegration (11:1-9).

The primeval history presents a view of history in which creation is shown to have a purpose in terms of God's intention to bless humanity. A tendency on people's part to resist his purpose is met both by acts of judgment but also by acts of grace. The first creation intention remains intact at the close of this part of the story. The intention of the narrative to speak to the community of Israel with contemporary relevance may be observed in two details: first, the explanation of marriage contained in the second creation account (2:24-25), and second, the contemptuous allusion to Babylon in the Tower of Babel incident. The latter reveals much about the nature and intention of Gen 1-11. Babylon not only became, in time, an oppressor of Israel, but it also had creation and flood narratives of its own, which explained the world in terms which claimed the supremacy of itself and its gods. The Old Testament's primeval history, with its doctrine of one supreme God, has sharp teeth in the context of its contemporary intellectual and political world.

The patriarchal narratives begin, strictly, within Gen 11, with the announcement of the story of the family of Terah, the father of Abraham, or Abram, as he is initially called (11:27). The key passage, however, is 12:1-3, in which Abraham has his decisive encounter with God. These verses mark the beginning of a narrative which continues well beyond Genesis, in the story of the 'great nation' promised here as Abraham's offspring. The remainder of Genesis may be seen as the beginning of the fulfilment of the promise, with obstacles first set against it, then overcome. First, Abraham's own son Isaac is born (and miraculously saved from death, Gen 21-22), then the sons of Isaac, namely Jacob and Esau (25:19-26), and finally the twelve sons of Jacob (also known as 'Israel'), who become the ancestors of the twelve tribes. Throughout this story, with its many famous incidents, the motif of the promise is maintained and frequently repeated (e.g. 26:3-4; 28:13-14). The element of God's choice is also to the fore, in the selection of Isaac, not Ishmael (17:18-19), and of Jacob, not Esau (Gen 27-28), to be the bearer of the promise. The theological concept of covenant is used here (as in the primeval history) to characterize the relationship between God and the family of Abraham (Gen 15:18; 17:2).

This section of Genesis culminates in the story of Joseph (Gen 37-50), which may be seen as fulfilling the first part of the promise to Abraham, in establishing his descendants as a substantial people, and even, through Joseph's wisdom, in making the people a blessing to the 'nations' (in the shape of Egypt). In the context of the larger Pentateuchal narrative, Genesis shows that the God who created was the same God who met and chose Abraham, to whom he was known by the name El; and that this God was none other than Yahweh, who in time would make a covenant with Israel.

Exodus

The Book of Exodus continues the important themes established in Genesis. It has at its heart the meeting between Yahweh and Israel at Mt. Sinai, following the exodus from Egypt. The main divisions of the book are: i) Exod 1-18: the call of Moses, plagues, Passover and exodus; ii) Exod 19-24: the making of the covenant at Sinai; iii) the making of the Tabernacle and consecration of priests (Exod 25-31, 35-40); iv) the apostasy at Sinai (Exod 32-34).

The dominant idea in Exodus is the presence of Yahweh. This is established already in the context of the call of Moses, which has the function of giving credentials not only to the great leader, but also to Yahweh himself. Yahweh now makes himself known to Israel, through Moses, by declaring that he is the same God who was known to their ancestors (3:13-15). The subsequent narrative of the plagues on Egypt can be understood as the sequel to this affirmation, for it pits the power of Yahweh against that of Pharaoh and Egypt in a series of trials which culminate in the death of every firstborn in the land, except Israelite children.

This 'Passover' is presented in Exodus as one of the key moments in Israel's history. The account of it shows this very clearly, for it is not only a relating of the events, but at the same time it constitutes a prescription for all future memorials of the event in the Passover feast (Exod 12:1-28; notice the provision for passing on the reason for the feast to successive generations, vv. 26-27). Once again the Pentateuchal narrative is shown to be not just history but authoritative religious text. The first part of the book ends triumphantly with the Song of the Sea, Exodus 15, celebrating Yahweh's victory over his enemies.

A key motif in the story of the plagues and Passover was Yahweh's intention, in his plan to save Israel, that they should worship him (Exod

5:1; 8:1). This is now fulfilled in the next major division, Exodus 19-24, in which Israel gathers before Yahweh at Mt. Sinai, to enter solemnly into a covenant which will establish them as his people.

Exodus 19-24 is one of the key texts in the entire Old Testament. In it, God enters solemnly into a covenant with his people. The passage is the Bible's account of the foundation of the nation of Israel. It consists of an awe-inspiring encounter between God and Israel, in which the liberation from Egypt is recalled as a basis of the new relationship (Exod 19, especially vv. 5-6); a setting out of the terms of the relationship, including the well-known Ten Commandments, or Decalogue (Exod 20:1-17) as well as other laws, (Exod 20:18-23:33, often known as the Book of the Covenant); an agreement to these terms on Israel's part (Exod 19:7; 24:3, 7); and a sealing of the agreement by a sacrificial ritual. These elements are typical of ancient near eastern covenants and treaties (see Old Testament World, Chapter 1).

Israel is thus now bound in a loyalty relationship with Yahweh. The significance of the covenant or treaty-form of the foundation events is that Israel is dependent for all its life on Yahweh alone. This applies to religion, politics and society, all of which were typically linked in the ancient world. In this way, not only is the worship of other gods prohibited (the cardinal rule for Israel's life, Exod 20:3), but also the sort of religious–political arrangements which always went along with them, whether in Egypt, Canaan or Mesopotamia. These cults were royal; that is, they were controlled by kings in feudal systems. Israel's king is Yahweh, and its laws resist the monarchical politics of other nations.

The Laws in Exodus

This explains the importance of law at this point in the Pentateuchal narrative, the decalogue and the Book of the Covenant occupying between them the bulk of the Sinai section. In fact, the Book of the Covenant is the first of three major law-codes in the Pentateuch, perhaps the fundamental one (the others are the Holiness Code, Leviticus 17-26, and the Deuteronomic Code, Deuteronomy 12-26). If the covenant at Sinai is a kind of legal constitution, establishing Yahweh as Israel's king, then it is not surprising that it should be regulated by law; kings are often cast in the role of lawmaker in the ancient world.

The relationship between the Decalogue and the Book of the Covenant that follows it is like that of a basic charter to specific laws.

The specific laws work out in detail the provisions of the basic law. For example, while the Decalogue categorically forbids murder (Exod 20:13), it is left to the law-code to work out distinctions between murder and accident, and to make provisions accordingly (Exod 21:12-14). While the Decalogue prohibits stealing (Exod 20:15), the Book of the Covenant works out further what might be implied in that prohibition, as when someone lets his cattle graze another's field (Exod 22:5).

Such provisions move into the realm of what we call 'civil law'. And the distinction between the Decalogue and the law-codes has sometimes been seen to be like our distinction between criminal and civil law. This is not quite suitable, however. Rather, the law-codes show how a basic set of requirements is elaborated in specific situations. (How this related to the legal processes is not quite clear; we made some comments about it when thinking about the Old Testament World; Chapter 1.)

This grey area that existed between secular and religious is typical of the Old Testament's thought world. The Decalogue itself expresses Israel's duty first of all to Yahweh, in the first four 'commandments' (Exod 20:2-11), and moves then to social regulations. A new short set of laws, given after the sin of the Golden Calf (Exod 32) and sometimes called the 'ritual decalogue' (Exod 34:17-26) emphasizes religious obedience even more. Likewise, the Book of the Covenant passes easily from laws regulating social behaviour to laws in the area of worship (e.g. Exod 22:29-30), and indeed contains the oldest law on the three major annual festivals in Israel: Passover (not named as such here, but connected with Unleavened Bread, which is), Harvest (i.e. early harvest, or Pentecost), and Tabernacles (late harvest, also known as Booths; Exod 23:14-18).

The mix between secular and religious may be understood theologically as a consequence of Yahweh's sovereignty in all of Israel's life. The authority behind the laws resides in his person. In this respect biblical law differs from ancient Near Eastern law, which takes its authority more directly from the king, and less so from the gods.

Sinai and Worship

The meeting with Yahweh at Sinai has an important worship dimension to it (the people must 'consecrate' themselves for the encounter; Exod 19:10-11); and it finishes with sacrifice (24:5-8). And as other gods demand worship of their people, so will Yahweh. This is why the story now moves to the instructions for building a 'tabernacle', or tent-sanctuary, for Israel's ongoing worship of him (Exod 25-31). These instructions include the making of the tent itself, as well as an outer surround for it, the altar and other furnishings, the consecration of these, and finally the consecration of Aaron and his sons, for all time, as priests. Chapters 25-31 contain the instructions; the execution of them is related in chapters 35-40. The book closes with a picture of Israel gathered around the tabernacle. It is essentially mobile, for the people have to go on a journey. The journeying is that of a worshipping people going with their God to a destination that he is showing them. His presence with them – the great theme of Exodus – is symbolized by the cloud that covers the tabernacle by day, and the fire that was in it by night (40:34-38). The same imagery fits into the theme of God's guidance; for it is the lifting of the cloud that serves as the signal to move forward towards the promised land.

The Breach of the Covenant

One other 'cloud', of a different type, is on the horizon in Exodus, however, and that is the subject of Exodus 32-34. This concerns the famous incident of the 'Golden Calf' which the Israelites made, under Aaron's leadership, while Moses was still on the mountain receiving the commandments from God. The making of the calf is presented as a great act of idolatry, a making of 'gods' (32:1). It is therefore a breach of the first commandment (20:3) right at the moment when the covenant is being made. This act of rebellion against Yahweh is one of the decisive moments in the narrative. In recording it, the Old Testament avoids all triumphalism in the foundation story of Israel. The covenant people show their religious and moral weakness from the beginning. And their failure throws into question the whole existence of the covenant. Can there be a covenant, or loyalty-relationship, between God and Israel at all, when Israel shows itself from the outset to be prone to disloyalty (33:3)?

The outcome of the story is a resolution of this tension, for Yahweh hears Moses' prayer that he should forgive them and continue with them. The stone tables of the covenant which he broke when he first saw the people's sin (32:19) are therefore remade (34:1-4), and the covenant is maintained, explicitly on the basis of God's mercy (34:6).

At the end of Exodus, therefore, a new stage in the accomplishment of the promise is complete. God has entered a relationship with his people. But there is a sombre undertone to the story, for the relationship has been shown to depend on God's readiness to forgive the sin of the people. Exodus as a whole shows its permanent relevance to the life of the worshipping community, not only because of its Passover regulations, but also because of its commandments and laws, and perhaps most importantly, because of its analysis of the religious condition of the people of God.

Leviticus

Leviticus is the paradox of the Pentateuch. At face value it seems obscure and remote from the modern reader's life. Yet it occupies a key central place in the Pentateuchal schema, the mid-point of the five books. The dominant idea in the book is that of 'holiness'. The covenant people are to be a 'holy' people. This idea has important visible dimensions. The people's holiness is marked by special times set aside for worship (cf. Exod 23:14-17); special personnel assigned to care for the worship life of the community (principally the priests, cf. Exod 28-29); special actions carried out in the worship (mainly sacrifices), and special places at which holy activities may be pursued, here the tabernacle alone. Leviticus contains rules on specific sacrifices (Lev 1-7); more on consecrating the priests and purifying the tabernacle (Lev 8-10); regulations about ritual 'uncleanness' (11-16), and laws concerning holy living (17-27).

These laws (Lev 17-27) constitute the second major law-code in the Pentateuch, the so-called Holiness Code, named because of the characteristic motivation to obedience: 'You shall be holy, for I the LORD your God am holy' (Lev 19:2). The mix of religious and social regulation is evident here as in the Book of the Covenant, well illustrated in Leviticus 19. The dominant note of holiness, however, serves to underline the origin of all authority in Israel in Yahweh himself.

Right at the heart of Leviticus stand the laws for the 'Day of Atonement', (Lev 16). This was the one day of the year when the High Priest, and he alone, might enter the most holy part of the tabernacle, the 'holy of holies', and make sacrifice there for the sins of all the people.

The significance of Leviticus in the Biblical narrative is immense. It characterizes God's people as a holy people, marked out for his worship. It makes worship a central idea in understanding the nature of the people's relationship with God. And if Leviticus stands at the heart of the Pentateuch, its own heart is the Day of Atonement. The Pentateuch as a whole, therefore, is shown to have this as its most prominent concern: the continuing life of the covenant people before God, and the maintaining of a healthy relationship with him. In its focus on holiness, grace and forgiveness, it continues themes which were introduced in Exodus.

Numbers

The Hebrew Bible's name for this book, 'In the Wilderness' (actually the opening words of the book), catches its theme more accurately than the English name. Numbers charts the journey of the people away from Sinai, its years in the harsh terrain of the Sinai peninsula, and its approach at last to the promised land of Canaan. The almost symmetrical balance with the Book of Exodus may be seen at once. As Exodus took Israel from Egypt into the wilderness and to Sinai, so Numbers takes them from Sinai, back into the wilderness and on to the verge of Canaan. Both the holiness theme and the narrative threads are developed here. By this stage in the Pentateuchal drama, Israel has its tabernacle and its laws for maintaining fellowship with God. Exodus had signalled that the Israelites would proceed as a people gathered round the tent-shrine (Exod 40:34-37). This provision is now embodied in the detailed picture of the tribes distributed in a special arrangement around the tabernacle as it moves off on its journey. The procession of Israel on its way is a procession of the Lord, Yahweh himself, attended by his people. They are now, however, not only a cultic (or worshipping) assembly, but also an army. Yahweh marches on the land which he will take as a warrior, and give to his people. This is the significance of Numbers 1-10.

The narrative strand focuses on the journey itself and the difficulties which lie along the way. The chief difficulty arises, as it did at Sinai, in the nature of Israel, this time in its failure to take the land at first approach, because of its fear and lack of faith in Yahweh (Num 13-14). It is as a consequence of this that they are condemned to a long spell in the wilderness, though the sojourn there could have been short (Num 13:25-33; 14:20-23). Here as at Sinai, it is only the intercession of Moses (14:13-19) which prevents a greater punishment.

The narrative continues, however, with Israel's eventual progress towards its goal, negotiating its way along southern and eastern boundaries of Canaan (Num 20-21). The account narrates at this point the people's first military victories, over King Sihon of Heshbon and Og, king of Bashan (Num 21:21-35). This gives good hope that the promise will in the end be fulfilled. A key passage now follows in the story of Balaam, a sorcerer whom Balak, King of Moab, tries to hire to cast a spell on Israel and thus prevent them from reaching the land (Num 22-24). Balaam knows, however, that Yahweh intends to bless his people, and therefore that he is powerless. It is a significant moment in the story of God's salvation of his people.

Embedded in this narrative is an oracle which foreshadows the later dominance of the tribe of Judah in Israel, a passage which has subsequently been interpreted messianically (Num 24:17). It may be compared with other Pentateuchal passages which show the purpose of God to bring ultimate victory out of potential disaster (Gen 3:15; 8:20-22; 22; Exod 34:9).

The remainder of Numbers contains a variety of material, including a census of the people (26) and additional rules about worship and other matters (28-30). The most significant topic, however, is that of preparation to occupy the land. Issues dealt with in this connection include the inheritance rights of women (27; 36); the settlement of the tribes of Reuben, Gad and half of the tribe of Manasseh in Transjordan, and the subsequent relationship of these tribes to those who would have to go over the Jordan to take their lands (32); the boundaries of the land (34); cities for the Levites (that is, the priestly tribe, which would have no land-inheritance of its own), and 'cities of refuge', for those who have committed manslaughter (35).

Numbers, therefore, anticipates the possession of the land in a comprehensive way. Typical of it is its combination of religious and military themes: the God who goes with his people, and whom they worship, is the divine warrior. This combination is symbolized in the pairing of two figures who represent the religious and military dimensions of Israel's life respectively, namely Eleazar and Joshua, who together will be responsible for apportioning the promised land (Num 34:17). They occur again together at the beginning of this task in Joshua 14:1, illustrating the important structural and thematic links between these two books.

In the closing stages of Numbers, the shadow of the land begins to fall heavily on the Pentateuchal narrative. But the people are not there yet.

Deuteronomy

More than any other book of the Pentateuch, Deuteronomy possesses a character of its own. It has a self-contained structure, which, as has often been pointed out, bears strong resemblances to many treaty texts of the ancient Near East. Consistently with this formal feature, it also arrests the flow of the narrative, which we have traced from the beginning of Genesis. The Israelites, having arrived at the plains of Moab, that is to say on the borders of the land, get no further in Deuteronomy; they remain there, to hear the last exhortations of Moses before they enter.

Deuteronomy is, of course, carefully fitted into the larger Pentateuchal narrative. For example, its final short section, the account of the death of Moses (Deut 34), recalls the earlier decision of God that he would not enter the land himself (Num 20:12). However, it is also in a sense self-standing, for it contains its own version of a number of elements in the earlier narrative. It retells the story of the exodus, the first failure to occupy the land, the approach via Edom and Moab, the victories over Sihon and Og, and the settlement of Reuben, Gad and half of Manasseh in Transjordan (Deut 1-3). It also recalls the encounter with God at Sinai (which it always calls Horeb; Deut 4-5), restates the Decalogue, with minor differences (Deut 5:6-21), relates the apostasy of the Golden Calf (Deut 9-10), and has its own law-code (12-26), which in places seems to be an elaboration of the Book of the Covenant (Exod 21-23). It is not surprising, therefore, that Deuteronomy should have acquired in the ancient Greek and Latin versions (the Septuagint and Vulgate) the name by which it is now known, meaning Second Law – even though this name is based on a mistranslation of the Hebrew of Deuteronomy 17:18 ('a copy of this law')!

Deuteronomy is by no means mere repetition, but has a distinct character of its own. This is often defined as a strong ethical, humanitarian tendency. The point can be illustrated by a comparison of the deuteronomic Decalogue and law-code with the corresponding parts of Exodus (Decalogue and the Book of the Covenant). In the Decalogue, for example, Deuteronomy presses home the command to allow servants to rest on the sabbath, by adding an extra clause (Deut 5:14). For the law-code, Deuteronomy's law of slave-release shows very well the kind of refinement that is made here by comparison with the Book of the Covenant. In Deuteronomy, the female slave stands on a par with the male (Deut 15:12, 18). Furthermore, when a slave is released, the one who releases must also provide him with means to resume an independent life (15:14). To call this emphasis 'humanitarian' is partly true. There is also a strong theological factor in play, however. It consists in the call to Israel to behave in a way consistent with its salvation by God from Egypt (15:15), and in an emphasis (correspondingly) on the 'brotherhood' of all Israelites (15:12).

Deuteronomy may be considered a preaching of the covenant. Its pervading idea is that the covenant once made at Horeb must be entered again by each new generation, hence its bold affirmation that the covenant was actually made with the new generation and not with its forbears (5:2-3). Deuteronomy focuses on the continuing covenant life of the community in all generations to come; the strong theme of teaching the constitutive events of the nation's history to children is to be understood in this light (6:6-9). So too is the provision for regular readings of 'the book of the law' (31:26, apparently Deuteronomy itself) at intervals in the nation's life (31:9-13). The supreme document of covenant theology in the Old Testament, therefore, is ultimately a document of covenant renewal.

Deuteronomy is also distinguished by its style, which has a strong hortatory flavour, employing rhythmical cadences, repetitions and a distinctive vocabulary. This is in keeping with its content and function, as an exhortation to live in covenant faithfulness, according to Israel's status as God's holy people (7:6-11). The effect of Deuteronomy's positioning as the last book in the Pentateuch is that all the history and traditions of Israel contained in the preceding four books are made to call Israel to faithfulness, in all its generations. The fact that it stops short of the story of the entry to the land may be intended as a powerful rhetorical device to show that Israel must always enter the covenant again, and the blessings of the covenant may never be taken for granted.

—— Authorship of the Pentateuch ——

We have now looked at the Pentateuch as if it were a single coherent story, as indeed, from one point of view, it is. Yet we cannot avoid the question of how it came into its present form. Indeed, we have already seen the hands of biblical authors at work, whether shaping a distinctively biblical account of the well known creation and flood traditions, or reflecting on the relationship between the Canaanite high god El and Israel's Yahweh, or applying the ancient Near Eastern concept of covenant to theology, or drawing on their environment again for their law-codes. We have even noticed different styles of writing; the sophisticated narrative techniques found in the Abraham stories, for example, where the question about the fulfilment of God's promise is effectively dramatized, and the rhetorical style of Deuteronomy.

Who, then, wrote these books? Was it one author or many? The question is complicated for many readers of the Bible by their proper respect for the impression that comes from the Bible itself, in this case that Moses was responsible for much of the Pentateuch. Yet even so, the question of authorship can hardly be avoided. Already in the early centuries of the Christian era astute readers felt that Moses could hardly have written the story of his own death (Deut 34). And in fact much of the Pentateuch writes about Moses in the third person; that is, someone else must be writing about him. So who did, and when?

The questions go deeper. Is the Pentateuch, after all, a coherent piece of writing? At the very least, it consists of quite different kinds of material: narrative, law-codes, instructions for sacrifice, exhortation. Deuteronomy seems to be a self-contained book with its own distinctive character.

There are also repetitions. Deuteronomy, for example, repeats material from Exodus-Numbers, and in a quite new way. And are there even different versions of events and incidents within certain parts of the Old Testament? There are two different creation narratives, as we saw (Gen 1:1-2:4a; 2:4b-3:24); two accounts of Moses finding water in the wilderness by striking a rock (Exod 17:1-7 and Num 20:1-13). And there are, as we have seen, several law-codes, often covering rather similar material.

In the nineteenth century scholars began in earnest to develop theories about the composition of books, that were explicitly free from constraints arising from religious convictions. A landmark study was that of the German scholar W. M. L. de Wette in 1805. De Wette was a theologian and preacher of some standing, but he believed that as a scholar he was free to come to independent conclusions about matters of dating and authorship. And he concluded on stylistic grounds that the Book of Deuteronomy must have come from a different time from the other books of the Pentateuch. He dated it to the time of King Josiah in the seventh century BCE, many centuries after Moses, and most scholars since then have followed suit.

The classical analysis of the Pentateuch was formulated in the 1870s by Julius Wellhausen. He believed that the Pentateuch consisted of four originally quite separate documents, each of which treated the origins of Israel in its own distinctive way. These, however, were finally woven into the single narrative that we now possess by compilers, or 'redactors' (to use the term that has become common in Old Testament studies). The four documents, known as J, E, D and P, dated from different times. J and E were named after the divine names Yahweh (Jahweh in German) and Elohim (God), because it was thought that each document more or less consistently preferred the one or the other. They originated in the early part of the monarchy period, and from different parts of Israel (south and north respectively). D was a form of Deuteronomy, and was identified with the 'Book of the Law' found by King Josiah during his reform of the worship of Judah in 621 BCE (2 Kgs 22:8). And P, finally, was a 'priestly' writing from the exile, or possibly the post-exilic time. In this way the composition of the Pentateuch was linked into what was known about the course of Israel's history from its early days in the 'promised land' to the exile. The diversity of form and content was explained by the theory that it was formed gradually over many years by many different hands.

We can illustrate the theory by turning again to the creation accounts in Genesis 1-3. According to the Documentary Hypothesis (as it came to be known) the first creation narrative (Gen 1:1-2:4a) was attributed to the source P, and thus the exilic period, while the second (2:4b-3:24) was actually earlier, being part of the J source, from the time of King David. The point was not merely that there were two accounts, but that they differed in important ways. Genesis 1 tells of the making of the heavens and the earth, then of the creation of human beings, male and female (Gen 1:26-28). At the end of the famous account of the creation in seven days, however, there seems to be a new start. Here the earth is again pictured without human beings (Gen 2:5); the man is created before vegetation, (2:7-9; in contrast to 1:11-12, 26-28), and the creation of the man and the woman is separated by that of both vegetation and the animals (Gen 2:18-23). J was thought to have a simpler, or more 'primitive' view of God (a God who 'walked in the garden', Gen 3:8), while P, through the chastening of exile, and its close encounter with other nations, had developed a more sophisticated concept, the cosmic God of Genesis 1. In this way, the connections between Genesis and other creation (and flood) narratives which we have already noticed could be explained by a particular theory, namely that Israel had come into contact with Babylonian ideas during the exile, and shaped its own literature accordingly.

Other 'doublets' (that is, apparently duplicate accounts of the same incident) seemed to confirm that this way of thinking was correct. In the case of the water brought out of the rock, Numbers 20:1-13 has a consistently greater interest in 'priestly' things than Exodus 17:1-7 (Aaron, the tabernacle, the 'glory' of the LORD), and could thus be attributed to P, while the Exodus passage was traced to J.

One of the most important implications of Wellhausen's work was in the area of theology. He saw the Pentateuch as diverse not simply at the level of style and composition but also at this deeper level. The main distinction in this respect was between theology that was essentially 'priestly', that is, concerned with matters of priests, sacrificial worship, ritual holiness and atonement (as is typical in Leviticus), and on the other hand, ethical religion, typified by Deuteronomy. Modern scholarship has developed in different and important ways from Wellhausen's documentary theory, and we shall return to this. However, the four sources are often still referred to in scholarly work on the Pentateuch, even if they are now rather differently understood. And the broad distinction between ritual and ethical religion has proved particularly durable.

The Prophets

Under this second of the Hebrew Bible's three subdivisions is contained not only the books which are known to Christian readers as the prophetic books, but also those which may loosely be called the history books (Joshua, Judges, Samuel and Kings; Ruth comes in the Writings section, as do Chronicles, Ezra, Nehemiah and Esther). These history books are known to Jewish tradition as the 'Former Prophets', to distinguish them from the Latter Prophets (Isaiah etc.) A theological point is made by this similar designation of the two blocks of material: that is, both types share the theme of Yahweh's authority in history, and the judgment that comes on the covenant people when they are unfaithful to the covenant.

The Former Prophets (Joshua – Kings)

It is clear from the opening verses of Joshua that it does not mark a radical new beginning when compared with the Pentateuch. On the contrary, it continues the narrative which finished there with the death of Moses (Deut 34, cf. Josh 1:1). And we noticed a few pages back that themes surrounding the movement of Israel towards its land would be resumed in Joshua. The connections between the narrative of the

Pentateuch and that of Joshua are so pronounced that many scholars have wanted to speak of a 'Hexateuch' rather than a Pentateuch, pointing out that it is only in Joshua that the promise of land made to Abraham (Gen 12:1-3) is finally fulfilled. At the level of the narrative this point must be conceded. Indeed, there is no point in the story of Israel which can properly be called a conclusion anywhere between Genesis and the end of 2 Kings, when the people of Judah are transported to exile in Babylon.

There are also, however, strong thematic and theological connections between Deuteronomy and the books which follow (Joshua – Kings). For this reason, these have been called the Deuteronomic (or Deuteronomistic) History. So there are two quite different theories about the composition of Genesis – Kings ('Hexateuch' and 'Deuteronomic History',) The two points of view draw attention to different features of the larger narrative. Neither can claim to account for the material exclusively. (Indeed there is a certain trend nowadays to think of Genesis – Kings as a single foundation narrative of Israel.)

The designation 'Deuteronomic' is nevertheless helpful as a way of thinking of Joshua – Kings, for it highlights the fact that it is a covenant history. Joshua tells of the entry to the land, as a continuation of the divine warrior theme begun in Numbers. The combination of military and liturgical motifs surfaces here too, now in the central place which the ark of the covenant has in the narrative of the entry to Canaan (Josh 3-6). The conquest is a triumphal procession of God and his people together. The idea of the land and its people as *herem*, a thing devoted to God, even a kind of sacrifice, lies behind the stories of the destruction of Jericho and Ai (Josh 6:17; cf. Deut 2:34). The possession of the heartland of Canaan is marked by the fulfilment of a command made in Deuteronomy (27:1-7) to carry out a covenant renewal on Mounts Gerizim and Ebal, at Shechem in the northern highlands (Josh 8:30-35). And the main part of the remaining narrative tells of the division of the land among the tribes, finishing with further covenant renewals in the closing chapters (Josh 23-24).

If Joshua puts a predominantly positive light on Israel's early days in the land, the Book of Judges (like Exodus) ensures that there can be no triumphalism. It relates to the days between Israel's arrival in the land and the rise of the monarchy. And its theme is the conflict between Yahweh's persistent will to save his people and their own tendency to fall foul of him because of unfaithfulness. Historically, it assumes a situation in which they do not hold the land either fully or with any stability. A pattern of gain and loss is built into the structure of the book. Repeated failure is followed by repentance and crying to the Lord, and is met by repeated acts of salvation, in which a succession of charismatic deliverers play their part. The pattern is stated programmatically in Judges 2:11-23. It has been called 'cyclical', but this is not strictly accurate, for there is a strong underlying tendency for matters to go from bad to worse, and at the end of the book Israel appears to have a very precarious hold on its land.

Joshua and Judges together seem to offer two sides of a story. On the one hand God is faithful to his promises, and has brought his people into the land as promised; the covenant history goes on. On the other hand, that history is always endangered by the very character of the covenant people. The 'history', therefore, is highly theological, as its designation Former Prophets suggests.

An important turning-point in the story of Israel in the land comes with the end of Judges and the beginning of Samuel. The historical issues behind the story have been outlined in the previous chapter. These include the transition from a tribal administration of Israel, in which charismatic 'judges' occasionally unite Israel for the purposes of defence, to a monarchy. We saw how the Books of Samuel portrayed the rivalry between Saul and David, David's final success in uniting the north and south of the country, the importance of the choice of Jerusalem as his political and religious capital, and the religious changes which were subtly brought in with what has come to be known as the 'Davidic covenant' (2 Sam 7: 23-5).

The division of the Books of Samuel into two is somewhat artificial, and is traceable only as far back as the Septuagint (the Greek translation of the Old Testament). Both are dominated by the figure of David. This is so (at least with hindsight) even from Hannah's Song, in which she praises the Lord following the birth of her son Samuel, and says:

he will give strength to his king,

and exalt the power of his anointed' (1 Sam 2:10)

This anticipation of David, preceding even the stories concerning Samuel and Saul, is matched by the celebrations of his kingship at the end of the book (2 Sam 22; 23:1-7). The promise of an everlasting dynasty, therefore (2 Sam 7), is a central point in a composition that finds its coherence in the figure of David.

There are, of course, phases in the narrative. 1 Samuel 1-15 is the first phase, relating the acceptance of kingship in principle, with the failure of Saul to match the requirements. The second half of 1 Samuel, chapters 16-31, concerns what has been called 'the rise of David', and includes the account of his choice by God (1 Sam 16), as well as pointers to his growing leadership potential in Israel (1 Sam 18:7), his evasion of death at the hands of Saul, and Saul's death at the hands of the Philistines (1 Sam 31). 2 Samuel catalogues, first, the war between the followers of Saul and David (2 Sam 2-4), David's accession as king of all Israel and his capture of Jerusalem (2 Sam 5), his bringing of the ark in triumph into the city (2 Sam 6), his establishment as king (2 Sam 7-8), a lengthy narrative of the course of his reign, which shows the difficulty he experienced, partly through his own character defects, in maintaining just and wise rule (2 Sam 9-20), and a final short section which returns to some of these themes, and has often been termed an 'Appendix' to the book.

These phases have been thought to reflect originally separate source-narratives: for example, an ark-narrative, which may have comprised parts of 1 Samuel (1 Sam 4-6) as well as 2 Samuel 6. The 'Rise of David' may have constituted another. And 2 Samuel 9-20, together with 1 Kings 1-2, has long been known to scholarship as the 'Succession Narrative', in the belief that it was once a separate account of the circumstances leading up to David's replacement on the throne by his son Solomon. These theories highlight the fact that the book contains a variety of literature. The so-called Succession Narrative, for example, has a style which matches well its theme of political intrigue. Particular theories, however, carry no certainty with them, and scholars differ on the exact limits of the sources that they suggest.

It is clear, on the other hand, that the book is the result of careful composition. The 'Appendix' features a 'ring-structure' (that is, it consists of six sections arranged as three matching pairs in a concentric pattern), designed to recall the pre-eminence of David and re-affirm the promise made to his house. It includes material which is chronologically displaced (2 Samuel 21 belongs in the time of the Philistine wars; 2 Samuel 24, with its identification of a place for the building of an altar, is probably to be dated before the bringing of the ark to the city (2 Sam 6)).

The Books of Samuel fit into the 'Deuteronomic' programme in the sense that they narrate the final taking of the land (hitherto certain enclaves, including Jerusalem, had always held out); now David has finally given Israel 'rest from its enemies' (2 Sam 7:1, cf. Deut 12:9-10) and also sought the place which the Lord has chosen for worship (cf. Deut 12:11).

Like Samuel, the Books of Kings were originally a single book, first divided into two by the Septuagint. They chart the history of the successors of David. The historical period covered is c. 970 (the accession of Solomon) to 562 BCE, the date of the release of the exiled King Jehoiachin from his Babylonian prison. Once again, we have already discussed the history of the period. But how do the Books of Kings present it?

In the context of the Deuteronomic History, Kings follows logically from Samuel, as it records events which are consequences of David's reign. Centrally, it tells of the progress of the covenant with Israel, now irreversibly mediated through the Davidic king. This is signalled at the outset, with a restatement of the promise, through David to Solomon – with the important addition that this covenant is now explicitly conditional (1 Kgs 2:4). Though there is this continuity, however, there is a clear development too. The books are somewhat different in character and style, in part because they cover a much longer period. Rather than the close focus of the Books of Samuel, Kings is more like a bird's-eye view, and its theology of history lies rather closer to the surface. For this reason, it has often been thought to convey more immediately than the other books (and Samuel in particular) the real interests of the Deuteronomic author.

The story of Solomon occupies 1 Kings 1-11; 1 Kings 12-2 Kings 17 recounts the history of the divided monarchy, that is, the parallel stories of Israel (the ten northern tribes, or 'northern kingdom') and Judah; and 2 Kings 18-25 recounts the last century of Judah's life, the time between the fall of the north and its own destruction by King Nebuchadrezzar.

The account of Solomon is ironically double-edged. He is portrayed as the wise king par excellence (1 Kgs 3-4), and the builder of the temple (1 Kgs 5-8); he is rich beyond compare because of the blessing of the Lord (1 Kgs 3:12-13). Yet at the end of his reign he commits apostasy (1 Kgs 11). This last chapter is crucial to the narrative, because it determines the division of the kingdom (1 Kgs 11:29-33), while implying that the future of Jerusalem and Judah is secure (1 Kgs 11:34-36).

The succession of kings, north and south, takes its cue from the later Solomon, for the story is largely one of unfaithfulness to Yahweh, in which the kings themselves take the lead and bear heavy responsibility. The northern kings are universally condemned, because they perpetuate Jeroboam's syncretistic state-cult (1 Kgs 12; cf. the verdict on Omri, 1 Kgs 16:26). With the southern kings the matter is more differentiated because some of them undertook reforms reinstating the worship of Yahweh (e.g. Asa, 1 Kgs 15:9-15). The formulaic introductions and conclusions to the reigns of individual kings provide the telling clue to the author's view and purpose here. The evaluation of Asa is a case in point, for it highlights reforming measures precisely in the area of worship (1 Kgs 15:12-13, 15); and even the important exception made regarding his piety is in the realm of worship (v. 14). Other kings who receive general praise are also censured in this one respect (2 Kgs 12:2-3).

The end of Kings also reveals much about its purpose. 2 Kings 17 explains the fall of the northern kingdom in terms of two things: first, an attachment to idolatry (vv. 9-10), and secondly, a refusal to listen to the prophets (vv. 13-14). This last feature is connected with language which strongly recalls the themes and style of Deuteronomy (vv. 15-17). The chapter illustrates well why these 'history books' were thought of as prophetic by the Jewish canonizers. And indeed, prophetic figures do loom large in the narrative (especially Elijah and Elisha, 1 Kgs 17-2 Kgs 9).

The final section of the book (2 Kgs 18-25) focuses on the two most important reforms of the period, those of Hezekiah and Josiah, and their failure, paradoxically, to prevent the fall of the kingdom. The ending of the book has puzzled some readers, because the reforms seem to correspond closely to the prescription of the Deuteronomist for survival. They have therefore suggested that an early form of the book closed with the narrative of Josiah's reform, and it was only chastened hindsight that prompted the continuation of the story down to the fall of the kingdom by a later, exilic writer. Alternatively, we may suppose that the writer of the whole book is exilic (as Noth did), and that he wanted to show that, even though reforms were carried out, the character of kings and nation was such that they could not finally keep covenant.

Conclusion

The Former Prophets as a whole, therefore, take the history of the people in the promised land up to what might appear to be the end of the story of God's covenant with Israel. This section of the Old Testament canon cannot be separated from the Pentateuch that preceded it. Not only does it continue the story (the Pentateuch lays the foundation for the covenant between God and Israel; the historical books show how it all worked out), but in a sense it brings it full circle. As Abraham had come from the 'land beyond the River (Euphrates)' (Josh 24:2-3), so now his descendants are taken back there in exile. From another point of view, the exile in Babylon echoes ironically the exodus from Egypt (Egypt and Babylon are morally the same, as we see in Joshua 24:14, and as may be inferred from Deuteronomy 28:68). The covenant has been broken; the formal 'curses' pronounced in

Deuteronomy's preaching (Deut 28) have come into effect.

It will be clear from the above that the authorship of these books must be complicated. The historical books no doubt contain traditions that recall Israel's actual early history in the land. The debates about kingship in Samuel, for example, make little sense if they are dated at a time after the monarchy has ended. These are echoes of real issues in the time when Israel as a tribal organization was giving way to the royal administrations initiated by David. Yet the books form a unity together which seems to take its meaning from the end of the story, namely the Babylonian exile. The Books of Kings both report events from long before and at the same time can reflect on the lessons to be learnt by Judah from the fall of the north – and ultimately that these lessons were not heeded. This means that the books are in some sense a compilation of old sources, by a writer or writers who had a theological purpose around the time of the exile. The main theories about this topic are considered in the following chapter. It is clear enough, however, that the books were formed as a result of careful and scholarly reflection on the past in the light of current events.

——————— The Prophetic Books ———————

These comprise the three major prophetic books, Isaiah, Jeremiah and Ezekiel, together with the twelve so-called 'Minor Prophets' (sometimes called the Book of the Twelve). The count excludes Daniel, which, though traditionally a 'prophet' in the Christian canonical arrangement, is not so considered in the Hebrew, where (with Ruth and others) the book is classed among the 'Writings'. In the Hebrew canon, the prophetic books follow immediately on the historical books (in keeping with the shared character of the two groups as implied by the names Former and Latter Prophets). This means that the books which intervene in the Christian Bible (from Chronicles to the Song of Solomon) do not appear at this stage in the Hebrew.

The arrangement of the books themselves is the same in the two canonical traditions (though Daniel and Lamentations have crept into the Christian list), and this shows that the books were considered a coherent group from an early point in the making of the canon. Some modern theories even suggest that the 'Book of the Twelve' was really considered to be a single book, though it is hard to demonstrate that this is so. Apparently primacy has been given to the longest books, which may in turn be ordered according to the chronology of the periods which they deal with (though the same theory cannot be applied to the Book of the Twelve).

The Prophetic Books and the History Books

Before we think about the message of the prophetic books, it will be worth noticing first some of the points in common between our books and the history books which we have just considered. One of the difficulties in reading the Old Testament occurs just at this point, for the connections between the books and the underlying history of Israel – which are obviously clearer in the case of the history books – are by no means on the surface here. A close reading soon reveals that the prophets are dealing with many of the same historical issues which faced the writers of the histories. In the account of Isaiah's meeting with King Ahaz, for example (Isa 7), it pays to cross-refer to 2 Kings 16 for some extra background to the events. That said, in the context of its own argument, the Book of Isaiah supplements the 'history-book' with additional narrative. Jeremiah does this also in connection with the time after the fall of Jerusalem, with material which does not occur in Kings (Jer 37-45). There are examples too of material that appears in both the histories and the prophetic books, sometimes in slightly different forms (Isa 36-39, cf. 2 Kgs 18-20; Jer 52, cf. 2 Kgs 25).

In subject matter and essential focus, there are also similarities. The two main periods around which the books cluster are the last decades of the life of Israel (the northern kingdom), that is, the middle of the eighth century, and the last decades of the life of Judah, a little over a century later. This is an important similarity with the historical books, especially Kings, which came to a twin climax in the telling of the fall of the north and south respectively. The prophets, like the history writers, are concerned with the big questions which attended the failure of the covenant. They also stage similar confrontations, involving king and prophet. As Nathan confronted David (2 Sam 12:1-15), and Elijah Ahab (1 Kgs 17-18), so now Isaiah faces Ahaz (Isa 7) and Hezekiah (Isa 22:8b-11 – though he is not expressly named), and Jeremiah challenges Jehoiakim and Zedekiah (Jer 36-39). The underlying issue is the same in all cases: will the kings lead the people in faithfulness to Yahweh and the covenant?

These similarities have caused some to think that the prophetic books have been given their final form by the same people who wrote the histories. If this were so, it would give interesting confirmation to the ancient Jews' perception that the 'Former and Latter Prophets' were indeed stamped with the same character. Unlike the Deuteronomic History, however, the prophetic books continue beyond the exile and even the restoration, bringing the prophets' challenge to the people in the new circumstances that prevail then (Haggai, Zechariah, Malachi).

The Prophetic Movement

We have noticed in general terms, both in preceding the chapter and in the remarks above, that the prophetic movement was one of the key features of Israel's religious history in the period of the monarchy. It was prophets who challenged wayward kings and people to return to the religion of Yahweh. Our task now is to consider more carefully the message of the prophets against its background, or backgrounds, and how that message came to be enshrined in the books which bear the prophets' names.

We have seen that both kingdoms, north and south, were built on religious foundations, in the Jerusalem temple and the sanctuaries of Jeroboam at Bethel and Dan. In the years that followed, religion and politics continued to go firmly hand in hand. The issue at all times was whether Israel would belong truly to Yahweh, or whether the two states would become effectively Canaanite.

The issue blew up already in the ninth century under Ahab, when Baal religion enjoyed official status because of Ahab's Phoenician wife Jezebel. The conflict at Carmel between the prophet Elijah and Jezebel's prophets of Baal sets the tone for the whole period. The depth of this clash of ideas is illustrated by the telling incident of Naboth's vineyard (1 Kgs 21). When Ahab uses force to acquire the other man's land, he acts like a tyrant. When Naboth resists him, claiming an inalienable right to the land because it is his 'inheritance' (1 Kgs 21:3), he appeals to the law and custom of the ancient tribal society. The old Israel, in which Yahweh was king, thus runs headlong into the new Israel, dominated by the power structures of Canaan. It is these conditions that give rise to the greatest phase of Israelite prophecy.

It was in the eighth century, which as we have seen, brought affluence to both kingdoms, that this movement reached the height of its creative power. There had always been prophets, apparently. A number of narratives in both the Pentateuch and the historical books suggest that they were originally some kind of ecstatic visionaries. Intermediaries of various kinds, between gods and human beings, were known in all the nations of the ancient world. On the basis of omens and other means, they gave oracles to kings concerning the likely outcomes of planned campaigns. There are hints of a function of this sort for the prophets of Israel in the Bible, and there seem to have been 'guilds' of prophets who constituted a professional class (2 Kgs 6:1). From these Ahab seeks reassurance before going to war with Syria (1 Kgs 22). And there were those who were ready to give such assurances, even if events proved that they had no sure grounds for doing so. Ahab's enquiry is a case in point. In the biblical narrative, not all the official prophets are considered false; in the Ahab incident, the truth is spoken by one of their number, Micaiah. Like Micaiah, the prophets whose work has come down to us were no time-servers, but courageous people who were prepared to put their lives on the line for what they considered the truth of Yahweh. The great figures of this classical period were Isaiah, Amos and Micah in Judah (though Amos preached in the north, at Bethel), and Hosea in the kingdom of Israel. It is not clear whether any of these were 'official' prophets, like those who advised Ahab. They appear to have come from different social brackets. Isaiah was a man of the court, but Amos was a farmer who denied that he was a prophet at all (Amos 7:14)!

Recent scholarship has shown interest in the 'social location' of prophets (see Wilson, Petersen). That is, it has tried to say to what extent the prophets had a central place in the political-religious establishment. It has found that prophets could be 'central' or 'peripheral' to society. This general point may be supported by the observations just made. In the Biblical picture, however, the issue is whether a prophet will bear the responsibility of speaking the truth, whatever the consequences might be for his relationship to authority.

The Message of the Prophets

Whatever the diversity of the prophet's origins, however, they were united by their message, which was directed essentially against two things: social injustice and false worship. Amos is characteristically scathing about the vain folly of the religion of his day:

Come to Bethel - and transgress; to Gilgal - and multiply transgression (4:4).

It is an ironic call to worship at popular sanctuaries, which says plainly that the worship that goes on there is nothing other than sin itself. He suggests elsewhere that it was actually idolatrous (Amos 5:25-27). And this theme is the main thrust of Hosea, who depicts the Baal worship of Israel as a kind of marital infidelity (Hos 2). Archaeology bears out that Israel was worshipping at a number of sanctuaries, and suggests that the worship there was not strictly Yahwistic. The altars discovered at sanctuaries in Megiddo and Beersheba resemble the altar of burnt-offering prescribed for Israel in that they possess 'horns' at the top four corners (Exod 27:2). Yet they were made of cut stone, which was forbidden by Israel's law (Exod 20:24-25). Moreover, statuettes of the goddess Astarte which have been found at Mizpah are among many artefacts which confirm the picture of mixed religion given by Hosea.

The theme of social injustice, the oppression of the weak by the strong, is sounded in some measure by all the prophets, perhaps most clearly by Amos. It is not coincidental that this should go together with the condemnation of unfaithfulness to Yahweh. For the two themes are combined in the ancient covenant. The laws in Exod 20-23 put right behaviour firmly in the context of loyalty to the God who has brought his people out of Egypt. The prophets, therefore, were motivated by one thing: a desire to turn Israel back to Yahweh alone, and to life according to his covenant. It is often observed that they do not often actually use the language of covenant. The covenant is implied, however, in the many assumptions they make that Israel was in a relationship with Yahweh that brought expectations with it (Hos 4:1-3; Mic 6:1-4). And in Hosea the concept is quite explicit (Hos 6:7; 8:1).

When the prophets castigate worship at the many sanctuaries of Israel, it might be thought that they are aiming to turn people back to the Davidic arrangement of a single royal temple at Jerusalem. In Amos' case there may be truth in this. When he tears a strip off the worship at Bethel it is bound to recall to the reader the account in Kings which sees the establishment of Jeroboam's official religion there as essentially idolatrous (1 Kgs 12). And he apparently foresaw the re-establishment of the Davidic kingdom (Amos 9:11-15). Hosea too hints that the making of kings in the north was fundamentally a false move, and seems to recall the sin of Jeroboam (Hos 8:4-5; 10:3-5). Yet this does not seem to be their main point. Amos is not crusading for a return to Jerusalem. Rather, he concentrates on the actual falseness of the religious practices of his day. It is clear on the other hand that sticking to orthodoxy by worshipping at Jerusalem is no guarantee that all is well either (Mic 3:9-12). The prophets go to the heart of religion; they seek a society that is based on truth, and a religion to match. It is a vision that protests deeply against the notion that there is effective power in holy places and actions in themselves. If this is the essence of Canaanite religion, then worship that bears the name of Yahweh is not immune from it. The prophets insist on the inwardness of religion, and in so doing have made their lasting contribution.

The Prophets as Preachers

The prophets communicated first and foremost in direct encounters with their contemporaries. The first striking thing about their discourse is its sublime form, often in an elevated poetic style which seems to have been one of the hallmarks of their practice. Some of the force of this, which depends on wordplays, alliteration and other devices, is not easily conveyed in translation. Yet the rhythms and persuasive power of the speech can still be appreciated. The following passage, describing the relentless advance of an enemy, makes the point:

He (Yahweh) will raise a signal for a nation far away,
and whistle for a people at the ends of the earth;
Here they come, swiftly, speedily!
None of them is weary, none stumbles, none slumbers or sleeps,
not a loincloth is loose, not a sandal-thong broken;
Their arrows are sharp, all their bows are bent,
their horses' hoofs seem like flint, and their wheels like the
whirlwind.   (Isa 5:26-28)

The vividness of this speech is achieved by features which are readily appreciated. Repetition is used freely to produce an intensifying effect. A special type of repetition is also on view here, namely 'poetic parallelism'. This, probably the most characteristic feature of Hebrew poetry, is a tendency for a phrase or idea to be echoed by a similar one closely following; the first two lines and the last two cited here exemplify this habit of mind, in slightly different ways.

Other features of Hebrew poetry are not so easily perceived in translation, but also had powerful rhetorical effect. A case in point is the phrase:

he expected justice, but saw bloodshed;
righteousness, but heard a cry.   (Isa 5:7)

The force of this depends on the fact that the words 'justice' and 'bloodshed' in Hebrew closely resemble each other, as do the terms 'righteousness' and 'cry'. The prophets, then, were skilled wordsmiths, and knew that the quality of speech could match the quality both of the thought and of the effect.

Not all prophetic speech is as intensely poetic as the examples quoted, and indeed translations often try to distinguish between speech in poetry and in prose. This is usually reasonably successful, although the distinction is not hard and fast, and even what passes as prose often has some of the rhythmical features of Hebrew poetry.

The prophets, then, were imposing speakers, and some of the key moments in the books are records of incidents in which their words produced a strong effect. Jeremiah preached in the temple area on an occasion when the people of Judah were flocking to worship (Jer 7:1-15), perhaps at one of the great annual feasts. He must have stood between the outer and inner courts of the temple, a point which everyone would have to pass. Jeremiah's excellent sense of occasion and opportunity says something important about the prophets whose message has survived. Their oratory was matched by their courage. On this same occasion Jeremiah narrowly escaped death, because of the anger of his hearers, who – religious people as they were – regarded his criticism of the official worship as virtually blasphemous (the story is told in Jeremiah 26:1-19). But another prophet, named Uriah – less famous but just as courageous – was not so fortunate (Jer 26:20-23).

Other prophets also made a stir. Amos ran across the religious officials when he preached at Bethel, one of the royal sanctuaries of the northern kingdom (Amos 7:10-13); he too had chosen times and places of worship in order to challenge Israel (4:4-5; 5:18-24). His contemporary Micah's criticism of the people and worship at Jerusalem had made such an impact that it was remembered a century later, and cited in the incident of Jeremiah's controversial sermon (Jer 26:18-19). Prophets were not averse to seeking attention in ways other than speech alone. Isaiah dramatized the exile of Egyptians and Ethiopians at the hands of the Assyrian empire by going naked for three years, in order to show that these nations were unworthy objects of Israel's hope and trust (Isa 20). And Ezekiel supported his preaching of the imminent destruction of Jerusalem by strange symbolic actions (Ezek 4-5).

The speech of the prophets had certain regular features, beyond its basic poetic or rhetorical form. Scholars often speak of the 'oracles' of the prophets, meaning utterances, usually relatively short, which have a particular characteristic. Many such oracles announce God's judgment (Oracles of Judgment). Obvious examples of this type are the numerous sayings beginning with 'Woe..!', such as:

Woe to those who draw iniquity with cords of falsehood,
    who draw sin as with cart ropes.   (Isa 5:18, RSV)

The 'Woe' saying, which here appears in a series, is a special type of judgment oracle, found several times in this part of Isaiah, and also in Amos (Amos 5:18-20; 6:1-7). There are many others. Some picture vividly the judgment which is coming (Jer 6:22-26). Others are extended arguments, aiming to persuade the hearers that their wickedness actually merits punishment (Amos 4:6-13). A special type of saying well illustrates this persuasive element of prophetic speech, namely the so-called 'lawsuit pattern'. The metaphor is based on the idea of a legal court, used to show that Israel is guilty of breaking its covenant commitment, while Yahweh in contrast has been faithful to his:

Hear the word of the LORD, O people of Israel,
for the LORD has an indictment against the inhabitants of the land.
There is no faithfulness or loyalty, and no knowledge of God in the land.
Swearing, lying and murder, and stealing and adultery break out;
bloodshed follows bloodshed.   (Hos 4:1-2)

and again:

Thus says the LORD:
What wrong did your ancestors find in me that they went far from me,
and went after worthless things, and became worthless themselves?   (Jer 2:5)

The lawsuit pattern shows clearly that the prophets presuppose a mutually accepted previous obligation on both parties, and that failure to meet that obligation has the most serious consequences.

The prophets, however, did not believe that God's judgment was the only possible outcome of the covenantal history. Alongside the Oracles of Judgment there were also calls to repent, and even promises of salvation. There was a time when many scholars believed that these were not authentic elements of the prophets' message, but this view is less widely found now than it used to be.

Calls to repent are interspersed in the prophets with the warnings about judgment. The key word is variously translated 'repent', 'turn', 'return', thus:

But as for you, return to your God,
hold fast to love and justice,
and wait continually for your God. (Hos 12:6)

The theme is developed at length in passages such as Hosea 14:1-7 and Jeremiah 3:11-14, 22. (In these passages there is extensive wordplay based on the basic verb 'turn', much of which is lost in translation.) The idea of repentance, however, is not confined to expressions which use the verb 'turn'. Amos exhorts his hearers to 'Seek the LORD and live' (Amos 5:6, cf. v.14). By this he means that they should stop worshipping Baal and begin again to worship Yahweh. Isaiah uses the language of faith and trust to make a similar point (Isa 7:9b).

In all the cases mentioned, the prophet evidently hopes that the people will heed the message and be saved from the punishment which will otherwise come. This thread in their preaching, indeed, puts the judgment preaching in its proper context, for it suggests that even that is intended not as a straightforward forecast of doom, but as a means to avoid catastrophe. (Hosea 12:6, for example, comes at the end of a passage which, taken on its own, seems simply to announce judgment; 12:2-5.)

Calls to repent are not in themselves promises of salvation, of course. Rather they put a choice before the people, which may or not have a successful outcome - and prophets were often pessimistic about this. Nevertheless, there are genuine Oracles of Salvation in our books. The one at the end of the Book of Amos (Amos 9:11-15) has often been thought not to have been part of the original prophecy, because Amos' message up to then has been so gloomy. However, its vision of a restoration of the empire of David is a likely enough expression of Amos' hope for a repentant Israel, and is nowadays increasingly seen as an integral part of the prophecy. Hosea too gives cause for hope in the midst of his proclamation of judgment. The famous passage in Hosea 11:8-9 promises a ceasing of Yahweh's anger on the basis of his compassionate character. And he too seems to foresee a Davidic restoration (Hos 3:5 – a passage whose authenticity, like that of Amos 9:11-15, has admittedly been disputed). Micah and Isaiah also have Oracles of Salvation, some of which are among the best known passages in the Old Testament (Isa 2:2-4 = Mic 4:1-4; Isa 9:2-7; 11:1-9; Mic. 5:2-6), embedded among more threatening texts.

Other books contain extensive promises of salvation, and as we turn to them the question of the larger context of the individual oracles will become prominent. Among the most famous is Jeremiah's New Covenant prophecy (Jer 31:31-34). This promises a 'covenant renewal' with a difference, for it will bring in a covenantal relationship between God and Israel which will be different in quality from the former Mosaic covenant. This promise recognizes the deep problem which Israel has had in keeping covenant in the past, and therefore announces a quite new act of God which will somehow ensure their future faithfulness. This will be achieved by his 'writing his laws on their hearts' (Jer 31:33), a guarantee therefore of a genuine inwardness in the people's future devotion.

The New Covenant must be understood as part of Jeremiah's wider vision for the future of the people. It is found in the section of the book known as the Book of Consolation, Jeremiah 30-33, which consists largely of assurances of a bright future for the people. It is important to realize that the promises are held out to the people of Jeremiah's day. The beneficiaries of the New Covenant are 'the house of Israel and the house of Judah' (Jer 31:31). The vision includes the rebuilding of the city of Jerusalem (Jer 31:38-40), which according to Jeremiah's primary message of judgment was soon to be destroyed by the Babylonians.

The Oracles of Salvation in this case, therefore, look forward to a time beyond the coming of the judgment which Jeremiah preaches at first. Their function is to keep the people from despair, by affirming that God is still the God of covenant and faithfulness, though he is about to bring punishment for Israel's (or rather Judah's) covenant failures. There is a view of history in this sequence which is well captured in Jeremiah 24. Here, the coming of the Babylonians is seen as a certainty, and as a decree of Yahweh to which his people must submit. If they do, there will be a future after the punishment.

Individual oracles in Jeremiah, therefore, must ultimately be understood in the context of a larger scheme that operates in the book as a whole. The present order (that is, the pre-exilic order, involving the Davidic king and the religious establishment associated with him) is passing away; a new order is coming. This revolution is illustrated well by Jeremiah 22-23. Jeremiah 22 catalogues the sins of the three kings who followed Josiah in Judah – Jehoahaz (here c alled Shallum), Jehoiakim and Jehoiachin (here called Coniah) – and declares that the historic dynasty which they represent is now at an end (Jer 22:30). The next passage, however, introduces the hope of a righteous king, also in some sense Davidic, who will one day rule in justice and righteousness (Jer 23:5-6). In this way, Jeremiah's vision of the new order embraces the hope that would come to be thought of as messianic. Parallel prophecies are to be found in Ezekiel 34:11-24; 36.

The most sustained note of promise in the prophetic books, however, is found in the Book of Isaiah, especially in Isaiah 40-55. These chapters have their setting after the time of Isaiah himself, and are almost always attributed to an unknown later prophet ('Second Isaiah', or 'Deutero-Isaiah'), who lived in Babylon during the time of the Jewish exile there. The prophecies in Isaiah 40-55 are dated to a time shortly before the end of the exile. Their burden is that Yahweh is about to act in a totally new and decisive way to save his people. This salvation will be like a new creation, and a new exodus (Isa 43:14-21).

With Deutero-Isaiah it is difficult to distinguish between the individual oracle and the argument of the whole collection. There is a sustained treatment of themes. The underlying idea is that of imminent deliverance from Babylon, and the restoration of the people to Zion. Supporting this is the theological argument that the catastrophe of exile was all part of Yahweh's purpose for his people; the punishment was to make atonement for past sin, but now that the atonement had been made, he was about to act in a new way for their salvation (Isa 40:1-2; 43:19). The argument is also apologetic or polemical, for it challenges the claims of the Babylonian gods that they are superior to all others, including Yahweh. These claims may have seemed rather convincing to the provincial Judeans who found themselves at the heart of the world's civilization, among mighty Babylon's great temples and palaces. Yahweh's speeches in this part of Isaiah, therefore, assert that he alone is king; there is none to compare with him (Isa 40:25-26; 41:21-24). The work which he is about to do will demonstrate this for all to see, when the idols of Bel and Nebo are carried off by a conqueror (Isa 46:1-2).

In the middle of this sustained theological argument come the passages known as the Servant Songs (Isa 42:1-4; 49:1-6; 50:4-9; 52:13-53:12). These do not fall neatly into any classification of prophetic oracles. They do, however, lend a depth to the theology of history that we find in Deutero-Isaiah, for they show that the salvation promised is not triumphalist, nor lightly won. The debate about who the servant is is ancient. He is equated with Israel (49:3), yet is typically presented as an individual. What may be acknowledged by all readers, however, is that the coming salvation is won at the cost of suffering.

The Prophets' Experience

We must now turn to the key question of the prophets' experience. Where did their message come from, and how did they know it was a true word from God? There are some clues to this. Isaiah evidently had a decisive experience in the Jerusalem temple (Isa 6). It is not clear whether this was his initial call. But it certainly shaped his understanding of his message and ministry. The experience was a vision of God, where the temple seems to have suggested the dwelling of God in heaven. The vision of God's holiness became the motive to Isaiah's prophetic activity. Other passages suggest that similar visions lay behind the ministry of prophets more generally. The experience of Micaiah (1 Kgs 22:19-23) is important because his vision prompts a particular oracle (unlike the case of Isaiah). Jeremiah too speaks of having stood 'in the council of the LORD', and makes this the test of true prophecy (Jer 23:18, 22). The vision of God, therefore, seems to have been important in the prophetic experience both at the level of basic self-understanding, and at least sometimes at the level of inspiring individual oracles.

In general, however, the prophetic books are quiet about the means by which God communicated with the prophets. The typical prelude to a prophetic saying is simply : 'The word of the LORD came to..', or variations of this (Hos 1:1; 3:1; 4:1; Jer 7:1; 13:1). This gives little away about the psychology of prophetic perception. Interestingly, though, the idea of hearing the word is sometimes mixed with that of 'seeing' (Isa 2:1; Amos 1:1), which may be a hint of the heavenly vision.

There is another dimension of prophetic experience, however, namely the involvement of the prophet himself in his ministry and its consequences. We have noticed already that prophets could perform signs to support their message, and these by their nature carried a personal cost (Isa 20; Ezek 3-4). Hosea was required to experience the unfaithfulness of a marriage partner in order to convey forcefully to his hearers the reality of their unfaithfulness to God (Hos 1, 3).

The classic case of prophetic experience, however, is that of Jeremiah. Jeremiah knew threats to his life from his own townsfolk (Jer 11:21-23; 18:18). He was forbidden to marry, as a sign of the coming desolation (Jer 16:2). He appeared actually to feel the pain which he said was coming on his people (Jer 4:19-22; 9:1). And above all, he expressed the anguish which his prophetic responsibility had brought him in a series of searingly honest prayers to God (e.g. Jer 11:18-20; 15:15-18), culminating in an expressed wish for death itself (Jer 20:14-18).

This is a crucially important feature of Biblical prophecy. It shows that prophecy is not conceived as just making statements, but that God's communication with his people is passionate. Both in Jeremiah's experience and the picture of the Suffering Servant of Isaiah, there is a suggestion that the pain of the human figure somehow reflects that of God himself over the broken relationship with his people. For example, his lament over his desolated 'heritage' seems to echo Jeremiah's grief at being an outcast in his home town (Jer 12:7-13; cf. 11:18-23; 12:1-6).

The Structure of Prophetic Books

We have seen in our discussion above that the prophets' sayings have been shaped and ordered in the process of the composition of the books as a whole. It is plain enough that there must have been such a process, distinct from the actual utterance of individual sayings. One of the difficulties of reading prophetic books, indeed, is to know where an original saying begins and ends, and how the various sayings have been linked together. At this stage, let us simply notice that there is a pattern in a number of the prophetic books. They exhibit a structure which moves from preliminary announcement of judgment with calls to repent, to a sense that judgment is inevitable, and finally to declarations of salvation at a point in the future. Hosea and Amos are cases in point, with their different closing pronouncements of God's determination to save the people in the end (Hos 14; Amos 9:11-15). Jeremiah embodies the structure on a grand scale, in ways that we have seen. And the Book of Isaiah, though widely held to be a composition of different prophets' words, illustrates the point in its own way.

The books, then, come close to expressing a theology of history, in which God affirms both his power and right to judge, and his resolve ultimately to save. The language and metaphors vary, reflecting the diverse experience of the different prophets. Thus Jeremiah thinks of a 'New Covenant', while Ezekiel has a vision of a new temple in centre stage (Ezek 40-48). The Book of Isaiah is memorable for its messianic promises (Isa 9:2-7; 11:1-9), and ideas of new creation and exodus. Yet there is a basic agreement at the heart of these images, with urgent words addressed to a contemporary audience balanced with visions of a better future which might be called 'eschatological' (relating to 'last things').

The Composition of Prophetic Books

If the prophetic books exhibit a certain structure, it remains to ask who was responsible for it. Was it the prophets themselves, organizing their own work in retrospect? A piece of narrative from Jeremiah may shed light on this question. In the fourth year of King Jehoiakim's reign (605 BCE) Jeremiah is told by Yahweh to write all his previous sayings on a scroll and have them read to the king (Jer 36:1-2). The king, on hearing them, cuts the scroll in pieces and burns it, and in consequence, Jeremiah makes a new scroll, adding words to it which were not on the first (Jer 36:32). This is the only picture in the Old Testament of a prophet exercising control over the ongoing use of his sayings, or returning to them. It suggests incidentally that prophets were capable of this kind of recall, and that they considered that their sayings, once given, were firmly established and had continuing validity.

It is not clear whether this incident sheds light on a process that was true for the formation of all the books. It may be that it is evidence only for the case of Jeremiah. Yet this instance does seem to suggest a way of looking at the whole question of the composition of the books. Jeremiah's ministry extended over a period of forty years or more. In that time, as we have seen, there was a development in his message. This is natural, in view of the changing circumstances during that time. And so we may suppose that there was ample opportunity for him to think at length about the message he had brought. The result might well be something rather like the book which we have at present, in one or other of its forms (MT or LXX). There is evidence, for example, in Jeremiah 3, that an original preaching of repentance has been overlaid by a perspective from a later stage in Jeremiah's life, when he was well aware of Judah's refusal to repent and the fact that the exile would actually happen. On this scenario, Jeremiah, with the help of his amanuensis (or scribe) Baruch, produced a 'redaction' of his own words in the form of a scroll or book, capable of being used and reused by the community of the faithful.

The closest parallel to Jeremiah is probably Hosea, for which a scenario similar to the one described here for Jeremiah has recently been suggested (G. I. Davies). In the case of Amos, it has been held that most of what constitutes his book might have been uttered within a relatively short space of time, during a single visit to the northern kingdom from his home and business in Tekoa. Isaiah is more complicated. If it is true that a large part of the book comes from 'Deutero-Isaiah' in Babylon, long after Isaiah of Jerusalem, a different kind of hypothesis is needed here. It is usual in modern study to suppose that the later prophet combined his words with those of his predecessor, perhaps even uttering them as a conscious development of his thought. Even here, however, the role of the prophet himself is seen as crucial in the production of the book.

The above scenario is a way of thinking about the process from individual saying to whole book. There is another rather different possibility, which is favoured by many Old Testament scholars.

This involves supposing that the prophet may have played little or no part in the formation of the book. The prophet's words are remembered and transmitted by the community rather than by himself. And indeed the community may have added further words and interpretations to the raw material that it received. Applied to Jeremiah (again the test-case) this means that in effect the book has been produced by Deuteronomists, a group akin to those who are held responsible for the final form of the History Books (the Deuteronomic, or Deuteronomistic History). There are indeed similarities of style and diction between these two bodies of literature, especially in the prose sections of Jeremiah. 'Deuteronomic' language is striking in, for example, Jeremiah 11:1-8. Even the account of Jehoiakim's burning of the scroll could be a deliberate echo of King Josiah's favourable reception of the 'book of the law' (2 Kgs 22-23), and a 'deuteronomic' composition. In one view, Jeremiah was composed in the exile in Babylon by a group who adapted Jeremiah's prophecies to the needs of the next generation (Nicholson).

The force of this second view of the composition of prophetic books is in the fact that they have indeed ultimately been preserved by the Jewish community that experienced the exile. Once the words of prophets addressed to urgent situations, they became in time 'scripture', collections of writings for the edification of worshipping communities. This change in the nature of prophetic words is most striking in the case of the northern prophets. Somehow the words of Hosea, spoken in the northern kingdom in the eighth century, must have survived the fall of that kingdom and been carried to the south, to be finally preserved there. Did southern scribes act as 'redactors', that is, alter or add to the final form of the book in the process of claiming it as scripture with up-to-date relevance? For example, could the hope expressed there of a new Davidic king (Hos 3:5) really be part of southern messianic expectation in the time of the Jewish exile? And might there be a similar explanation for Amos 9:11-15? According to this view the prophetic collections might have been quite extensively expanded by redactors, over a relatively lengthy period. They would have been responsible for the more or less regular pattern of the books. There is a formal dimension to this pattern (the superscriptions, giving the date and origins of the prophecy, would be an obvious instance). And there are similarities of structure and substance (as we noticed above). If this view is correct, the prophetic books are part of a highly developed theological programme for the community that has experienced the exile, and which has to think hard about its destiny in the light of that profound challenge to old theological beliefs.

Clearly these are two quite different ways of thinking of the composition of the prophetic books. They involve rather different fundamental evaluations of the material (for example, is the narrative of Jehoiakim's burning of Jeremiah's scroll a factual record or an invention to serve a theological purpose?). This in turn depends on how highly one evaluates the vitality of the prophetic tradition itself, and how independent it is in relation to the deuteronomic movement which some scholarship regards as all-embracing. The present author has tried to make a case elsewhere for the independence of the prophetic movement (*Judgment and Promise*). It may be, however, that the case of the prophetic books merely illustrates one of the dilemmas of reading the Old Testament.

The Writings

It is tempting to characterize this section of the Old Testament canon as simply all that is left! It includes books which, in the Christian canon, are distributed among the history books (Ruth, Chronicles, Ezra, Nehemiah, Esther), and the Prophets (Lamentations, Daniel), as well as the Book of Psalms, and books which are broadly known as Wisdom Literature (Proverbs, Job, Ecclesiastes, Song of Solomon). The reasons behind the formation of this section are not wholly clear, and a discussion of them belongs properly in the section on the canon (below). The distinguishing features of the section have something to do with the nature of the material (Psalms, the Wisdom books), and something to do with relative lateness in time (e.g. Chronicles – Ezra – Nehemiah).

Histories and Narratives

Chronicles – Ezra – Nehemiah

These books together constitute a history of Israel from its origins to a time well after the return of the Jews from their Babylonian exile. It is therefore to an extent parallel with Genesis – Kings. This is most obvious in relation to Samuel – Kings, as large parts of those books reappear, often verbatim, in Chronicles. Like the longer history,

Chronicles – Ezra – Nehemiah is a continuous narrative. This point is emphasized by the repetition at the beginning of Ezra of the last two verses of 2 Chronicles (2 Chr 36:22-23). Thus Chronicles takes the reader up to the end of the exile, and Ezra-Nehemiah reports subsequent events.

For this reason, and also because of shared thematic emphases, the three books (counting Chronicles as one) are often taken to be a single work, composed by 'the Chronicler'. The work is usually dated around 400 BCE (though sometimes later) and thought to be an encouragement of the small restored community to believe that they really are the inheritors of God's ancient promises to Israel. Thus the very high profile given to David, Solomon and the building of the temple in 1-2 Chronicles (1 Chr 11-2 Chr 9) reflects on the rebuilt temple. This may not be so grand in itself (Ezra 3:10-13), but it is the focus nonetheless of the promises to Israel. In this way, the Chronicler holds out hope of a great future for a small Jewish community dominated by a foreign power (now Persia). The prominence of David and Solomon in the work has led a number of interpreters to think that it holds out a 'messianic' hope.

Ezra – Nehemiah are important in their own right in the canonical literature. Some indeed see them as originally separate works from Chronicles, artificially joined to it. Their contribution to the Old Testament and later Judaism is bound up with the figure of Ezra, who appears in both books (Ezra 7-10; Neh 8). His mission, authorized by King Artaxerxes of Persia (Ezra 7:1-6), was to re-establish the primary place of the Torah in the life of the Jewish people. It complemented that of Nehemiah, whose special task was to rebuild the walls of Jerusalem, and secure a relative political independence for the Jews. The date of Ezra's mission was probably 458 BCE, while Nehemiah came in 444. (For the scholarly debate about their relative dates, see the discussion in Chapter 2).

Ezra's most famous act is perhaps his dissolution of marriages between Jews and non-Jews, contracted in the decades which had passed since the return from Babylon (Ezra 9-10). But his lasting significance is in providing for the teaching of the Torah. A window on this is afforded by Nehemiah 8, where the Torah is read at a great assembly, and not only read but interpreted for a people who, following years in Aramaic-speaking Babylon, now no longer understood the Hebrew language. Here we have a glimpse of the beginnings of the great Jewish tradition of scriptural interpretation, which would have its deposit ultimately in Targums, Midrash, Mishneh and Talmud. Not for nothing is Ezra remembered as the 'father of Judaism'. And the inclusion of his work in a section of the canon known as 'Writings' is perhaps very appropriate.

Esther

The Book of Esther tells a tiny part of the Old Testament story, but one which has an important place in the life of Judaism. In contrast to Ezra – Nehemiah, it tells of Jews who did not return from Babylon to Judea, but had become further scattered throughout the Persian Empire. Esther, indeed, becomes the queen of King Ahasuerus (Xerxes) – which might have shocked Ezra! But she uses her place to deliver her people from the evil machinations of a clever and ruthless enemy, Haman. It is not hard to see how this story – which can be read as an entertainment – has tremendously poignant echoes for Jews in the light of a history of anti-Semitic persecution.

Ruth

Ruth seems out of place in this company, telling a story, as it does, of a much earlier period, that of the judges. The story concerns a family from the Bethlehem area, who escaped a famine in Judah by going to live in Moab. In that land, the father dies, followed by his two sons, leaving his own widow, Naomi, and the Moabite widows of the sons. The story concerns the return of Naomi, with Ruth, one of the daughters-in-law, and their reinstatement in Judahite society, thanks to the honesty and generosity of their kinsman Boaz. The 'local colour' of the narrative is therefore ancient. The question of real historical setting, however, is not easily settled. The purpose of the book seems to hang on the last few verses, which show that David's ancestry was part Moabite. This might have fitted some ancient author's purpose. But it is also possible to read Ruth against the background of Jewish debates of the post-exilic period (either as an old story adapted, or as a free composition). In this case it might be a plea for a tolerant attitude towards non-Jews, or those of mixed ancestry. It would thus make an interesting contrast with Ezra. But it would not be far from the Book of Jonah, with its 'universalism' – that is, its message that non-Jews are not outside the range of God's mercy. (Jonah too is frequently regarded as a post-exilic work, being more akin to some of the other narratives in the Writings section of the Old Testament than to the prophetic books among which it stands.)

The Psalms and Lamentations

If the Bible is the 'word of God' to human beings, the Book of Psalms has a special place in it, because it is words of human beings to God. The Psalms derive from the worship of ancient Israel and of the Jews. Many of them probably originated in the temple at Jerusalem. This was certainly the opinion of the earliest collectors of the Psalms, who attributed a large number of them to David himself. But it is also held by most modern scholarship, because the Psalms have many allusions to kings and their role in Israel (Ps 20, for example, is a prayer for the king in battle). The Psalms therefore give a significant insight into the life of Israel in the important context of their worship of God.

Psalms sometimes accompany sacrifices. The heading of Psalm 100, for example, probably means: a Psalm for the Thank-Offering. Allusions to fulfilment of vows mean that the Psalmist is in the act of performing a sacrifice at the same time as he utters the Psalm (Ps. 22:25). The Psalms therefore show the other side of the coin from Leviticus, which contains regulations for the sacrifices (for the thank-offering see Lev 7:12-15, and for the vow-offering, Lev 7:16-17). The Psalms were also used, not surprisingly, at the great feasts of Israel. This is clearest in Psalm 81, which has express allusions to moments in the series of celebrations in the seventh month, including the Feast of Tabernacles (Lev 23:23-25, 34-36; cf. Ps. 81:1-5 – the allusions to the first and fifteenth days of the month in v. 3 make the link clear).

Some treatments of the Psalms have suggested that all of them had their original place in one or other of the main feasts, usually the Autumn festival (Feast of Tabernacles). This is variously seen as celebrating the renewal of the kingship of Yahweh (in a hypothetical ritual enthronement of the king), or simply as the festival of covenant-renewal. There is not enough evidence to prove specific theories of this sort however.

The study of the Psalms has attempted, however, to define more carefully the kinds of situation in which various Psalms might have been used. This has been done by means of so-called form-criticism (see below on types of criticism). Form-critical study attempts to describe types of literature and to understand the sort of settings in which they were typically used. In the case of the Psalms it was this line of enquiry which refocused attention from the question: Who wrote it? to the question: How was it used?

The main types of Psalms identified by form-criticism were hymns and laments. The hymn is the most common type of Psalm, being simply an expression of praise to Yahweh for his greatness and goodness. The short Psalm 117 illustrates the key features of the hymn: a call to praise, a reason or motive for the praise, and a repetition of the call. The hymns may be developed in a variety of ways. Psalm 104 is a hymn on the order of the created world, with echoes of Genesis 1. Psalm 29 extols Yahweh in ways which are reminiscent of attributes of the Canaanite god Baal, and may be a way of affirming that Yahweh truly has those characteristics which Baal-worshippers wrongly assign to their god. Other hymns are Psalms 8, 33, 46-48, 84, 95-100, 103-104, 134-136, 145-150.

The Lament is that sort of Psalm which openly protests about some misfortune which the Psalmist or the whole community is experiencing, and prays that God will deliver him (or them) from it. In the case of the individual, the misfortune might be illness (Ps 6, 13, 38, 88) or personal persecution or false accusation (Ps 7, 26, 27). Some guesswork is involved in determining the cause of the psalmist's problems. Other Individual Laments include Psalms 3-5, 13, 22, 35, 51, 54-57 and 59. Typical elements are the complaint itself, often combined with a plea for deliverance, and (frequently) a new-won sense of confidence that the prayer has been heard (Ps 6:8-10). This is sometimes attributed to a moment in the worship-service when a word of reassurance is spoken by a prophet. But this is an argument from silence, and presupposes a rather mechanical view of prayer. It is best to explain the new confidence as part of the effect of praying.

The Community Lament is illustrated by Psalms 12, 44, 74, 79, 80, 126 and 137. Common to these is a complaint on behalf of the whole people. In some cases the cause can only be guessed at. Others (Ps 74 and 137) are obviously occasioned by the destruction of Jerusalem and the experience of the Babylonian exile. Once again, the main elements are complaint and petition, often with memories of God's past acts on Israel's behalf as a kind of motivation for him to act.

A few Psalms are classified as Psalms of Thanksgiving (Ps 30, 32, 118 and 124), different from the Hymn in that it celebrates some particular act of deliverance. The well-known Psalm 23 is a Psalm of Confidence. Others are meditations on God's word or laws, seeing in this the way of life (Ps 1, 19 and 119). Some are known as Entrance Liturgies, presumably sung in connection with a ceremonial procession into the temple (Ps 24; 68:24-27). And a few recall the course of God's history with his people, making it a matter of both praise and confession (Ps 78; 105-106).

Viewed according to types in this way, the Psalms afford an insight into Israel's life. This, at any rate, is what form-criticism hopes to achieve, because it looks always for the setting in life (or *Sitz im Leben*, to use the German phrase of its first proponents). A 'Thanksgiving' presupposes some situation in which thanks are due. The Psalms themselves only hint at such situations, of course. And it is by no means certain that all Psalms in our Psalter had their origins in worship situations. Yet the connection between many Psalms and Israel's worship is clear enough.

Even so, the Psalms should not be thought of exclusively as the hymns of the ancient temple. For they obviously had a life apart from and beyond that setting. They survive, after all, in a 'book', as part of the Old Testament scriptures. And there are signs that the Psalter was intended to be read as such, for the edification of the reader. The first Psalm illustrates the point, for it sets the idea of meditating on God's law at the very beginning of the collection. There are other signs of a process of editing, such as the division of the Psalter into five 'books' (Psalms 1-41 constitute Book 1, etc.), the inclusion as whole units of what might have been smaller collections (e.g. the Psalms of Asaph, 73-83; the Songs of Ascent, 120-134), and the provision of headings or superscriptions, presumably designed to aid meditation on the Psalm in question (e.g. Ps 51). The movement from individual Psalm to book-length collection probably corresponds to the transition from a society centred on the temple before the exile to a society deprived of its temple and thrown back on its Scriptures. The production of the Book of Psalms, therefore, may be apart of the development of the Jewish synagogue, often located in the Babylonian exile.

Lamentations

The Book of Lamentations is traditionally associated with Jeremiah, and appears immediately after that prophet's book in the Christian canon. This is because of the subject matter of the book, that is, laments raised over Judah and Jerusalem in the aftermath of their destruction at the hands of the Babylonians. This recalled the figure of Jeremiah, 'the weeping prophet', who had lamented for his people. At times, indeed, the speaker in the Lamentations is an individual who seems to suffer on behalf of his people (Lam 3:1-21, 48-66), which makes the echo of Jeremiah uncannily clear. The attribution to the prophet remains merely traditional, however; there is no concrete evidence for his authorship.

Formally, the Lamentations stand close to the Psalms of Lament. They are a set of acrostic poems, that is, there is a verse for each of the twenty-two letters of the Hebrew alphabet, arranged in alphabetical order. (Lamentations 3 is an acrostic in triplicate, having three verses for each letter. Lamentations 5 is an exception, having twenty-two verses, but not in acrostic form.) The poems express the pain and grief of the Jews very starkly, complaining bitterly of God's merciless abandonment of them, and the excessive nature of the punishment (Lam 2:1-5, 20-22). Yet there is confession of guilt here too (Lam 1:8), and at the heart of the book a vision of God's ultimate mercy (Lam 3:21-33). The poems therefore are a wide-ranging response to terrible pain and humiliation. They are deeply poignant, not only because they resonate with all human situations where pain has gone almost too deep for words, but also because of the astonishing restraint and discipline of their poetic form. The poignancy of Lamentations lies in this tension between the savagery of the subject matter and the regularity and symmetries of the form, between the sense of abandonment and the sublime expression of faith in the midst of it.

The Wisdom Books

The Old Testament's Wisdom Books, strictly speaking, are Proverbs, Job and Ecclesiastes. 'Wisdom', however, is a widespread phenomenon both in the Old Testament and in the ancient world. It is a convenient umbrella term covering a wide range of intellectual enquiry in Israel and beyond. At the heart of Wisdom is simply a desire to understand the world. This included the knowledge that enabled human beings to accomplish things, the knowledge of the farmer, for example, whose skills and observations were essential to the growing of food (Isa 28:23-29). The practical guidance of the counsellor is another important branch of Wisdom. The ability of David's adviser Ahithophel, indeed, has given him a kind of professional status (2 Sam 16:23); his story is a tragic one, for when his advice is finally rejected, he takes his own life, (2 Sam 17:23). Joseph and Daniel have also been described as 'Wisdom' figures because they exemplify a range of talents, especially in the area of government.

Proverbs

While this kind of Wisdom is found in a range of Old Testament books, it is the Book of Proverbs that represents the systematic collection of it. The basic raw material of the book is the short saying, the 'proverb' proper. It takes various forms. Sometimes it is shrewd observation of the way in which people think:

'Bad, bad', says the buyer,

then goes away and boasts. (Prov 20:14)

This kind of proverb is sometimes based on comparison. The essence of a thing is disclosed by analogy with something familiar:

Like vinegar to the teeth and smoke to the eyes,

so are the lazy to their employers. (Prov 10:26)

Here mere observation shades over into instruction for living, based on certain values. The need for industry and self-help is a major theme:

Do not love sleep, or else you will come to poverty;

open your eyes and you will have plenty of bread. (Prov 20:13).

Proverbs for this reason has sometimes been called secular. Yet the concern for an orderly life which lies behind exhortations of this sort is hard to extricate from a religious view of life. Wisdom is close to righteousness and folly to wickedness; the mix lies close to the surface in Proverbs 15, for example.

Alongside the short proverb is a more extended kind of reflection, common in Proverbs 1-9. This seems to be a development of the genre as instruction, perhaps in the home, hence the parent–child relationship that is presupposed here (Prov 2:1; 3:1 etc.), or possibly in school. The themes are similar, however, with the need for application (Prov 6:6-11) going hand in hand with warnings about immoral living (Prov 2:16-19).

There is other literature resembling Proverbs in the ancient world, especially in Egypt. Books of instruction in Egypt date back to the third millennium BCE (the instruction of Ptah-Hotep). And a second millennium teacher, Amenenope, has entered Old Testament textbooks because his teaching bears a very strong resemblance to a section of the Book of Proverbs (Prov 22:17-23:11). This has led many to suppose that the biblical author is directly indebted to Amenenope at this point, although others have found the correspondences to be explained more by the common nature of the material than in plagiarism. Egyptian Wisdom, furthermore, is more oriented to the royal court than Israelite. The former is training for an élite; the latter is more democratic. Yet the point is unavoidable that Old Testament Wisdom is a part of streams of thought shared by neighbouring nations.

Job

There is a kind of Wisdom, however, which looks beyond practical knowledge to enquire into the nature of human existence – life, death and pain, justice and injustice. The classic text for this in the Old

Testament is the Book of Job. Job consists of a 'prologue', poetic cycle and epilogue. The prologue is set in heaven, and the centre of the action is the accusation of Job by the Satan, who is not yet the fully developed devil figure of later biblical literature, but simply a member of the heavenly court, in the role of the 'accuser'. The fact that Satan does not return at the end of the book, when the issues are resolved, shows that the issue is not as such the role of a personal devil in bringing suffering. The issue of the book, rather, is whether the righteous Job has pure motives in leading his innocent life, and whether he would be so godly if he suffered terrible afflictions (Job 1:8-12). Satan is given a free hand, and the consequent afflictions brought on Job are the background to the questions about his existence which follow.

The body of the book is formed by the poetic cycle (Job 3-37). Here Job has an extended dialogue with his three friends, Eliphaz, Bildad and Zophar. They argue with increasing vehemence that he must have sinned, and that God is punishing him, or chastening him. Job, however, protests his innocence, and his main concern throughout is to have an encounter with God, so that he might plead his case and be vindicated (Job 13:3). In optimistic moments he believes that this will happen (Job 19:25-29), though not before he has roundly accused God of toying cruelly with him (Job 7:17-21).

The power of the Book of Job is at different levels. Partly it consists in facing up to the horror of human suffering. Job 24 comes close to a general depiction of the suffering of the innocent. Partly, however, it consists in its passionate reasoning about guilt, innocence and suffering against the background of certain current explanations which apparently belonged to traditional Wisdom teaching (Bildad is a keen advocate of the Wisdom of past generations, Job 8). Indeed, the words of the friends often stand close to the perspectives on the moral order found in Proverbs, or even Deuteronomy. Job, however, is prepared to affirm what the traditions have no way of accommodating, that an innocent person should suffer for no reason at all that anyone can point to. (The reader knows, indeed, that Job is actually suffering because of his innocence.)

The epilogue, furthermore, does nothing to tie up the arguments between Job and his friends. It is dominated by speeches of Yahweh – whom, therefore, Job finally meets. The response of Yahweh seems in some ways unsatisfactory, since it merely surveys the complexity of the creation, and shows that Job cannot understand these things. Yahweh's speeches seem to rejoice in drawing attention to the great oddities of his world, the crocodile and the hippopotamus, and perhaps the whale. There is no rhyme or reason in a creation like this, the argument seems to say. Yet in their oblique way the speeches do affirm an order in the midst of what looks like chaos. Finally Job is willing to accept this (Job 42:1-5), he is said to have spoken rightly of God (Job 42:7), and his fortunes are restored.

In this way, Job airs issues which were also faced by others in the ancient world. A Babylonian work, 'I will praise the God of Wisdom' (*Ludlul bel nemeqi*), has been called 'the Babylonian Job' because of its similar theme (ANET, 434-437). In it, a man who, like Job, has been religiously observant, and a teacher among his people, is nevertheless plunged into illness and wretchedness. He laments the incomprehensibility of the gods, and the failure of any prayer or divination to help. Unlike the Book of Job, however, the poem becomes a celebration of the sufferer's healing by the god (Marduk). A large proportion of it is given over to this, and the text as a whole belongs within the literature of the Marduk cult in the Esagila temple in Babylon. While Job too has a restoration of the righteous sufferer, it occupies a more marginal place in the book. By comparison with the Babylonian work, Job is no straightforward defence of God (or 'theodicy'), nor a case of triumphalist Yahwism. Job faces the worst of human experience, and emerges from it in worship, yet with a sense of mystery and wonder.

Ecclesiastes

The last of the three wisdom books is Ecclesiastes, also known as Qoheleth, the Hebrew name for the 'preacher' whose thought is collected here. Despite the indirect allusions to Solomon ('the son of David, king in Jerusalem', Eccl 1:1), the work is usually dated to the post-exilic period, the light Solomonic dress being a way of establishing the type (or *genre*) of the book as Wisdom reflection. It has in common with Job the basic question about justice in the world and the knowability of God. However, whereas Job was the passionate quest of a sufferer who hammered the gates of heaven and believed that he would meet God and be vindicated, Qoheleth's thoughts are more detached, and reflect more generally on the remoteness of God from the world and human experience (Eccl 3:11).

If the unknowability of God is the theme, it is not surprising that the main contentions of traditional Wisdom should be called into question here. Where the sages of Proverbs believe that wisdom is to be cultivated and has immense value for life (Prov 1:2-6; 15:22), Qoheleth sees even wisdom as 'vain' (Eccl 1:16-18); Proverbs had advocated an industrious life as a key to well-being (Prov 6:6-11), but Qoheleth finds no sure reward for honest labour (Eccl 2:11; 6:1-2); most defiantly, whereas Proverbs believed that a good and pious life is properly rewarded by God (Prov 15:9, 25, 29), Qoheleth doubts even this, thinking that all come to the same end, great and small, good and evil (Eccl 3:18-22; 8:14).

Ecclesiastes is structured as an inner dialogue, in which the propositions of traditional Wisdom are aired, but only to be called in question (for example, Eccl 8:12-13, 14). Because of its structure, it is not easy to know where its 'last word' lies. Even the final two verses (Eccl 12:13-14), which argue for an orthodox approach to life and faith, could be read either as sitting in judgment on all that has gone before, or as itself called into question by it. Scholars in the past considered that the book might be an amalgamation of different authors' work, explaining its inner tensions in this way. It is more common nowadays, however, to see it as a unity, and a representative of a sceptical way of thinking within Judaism. Its dominant point of view may be represented in its agnostic invitation to enjoy life as the opportunity comes (Eccl 2:24), as one is powerless to affect one's destiny (Eccl 2:24; 9:7-9). The latter text, interestingly, is closely parallel to a passage in the great Gilgamesh epic (Tablet X, stanza 3; ANET, 90), an indication of Ecclesiastes' openness to the thought of the ancient world.

Indeed, like Proverbs and Job, Ecclesiastes has parallels in other ancient texts. Closest, perhaps, is 'A Dialogue about Human Misery', a Babylonian text known from the seventh century BCE (though it may be older; ANET, 438-440). It shares Qoheleth's themes of the injustices of life, where the wicked prosper and the weak go to the wall, religious observance brings no benefit, and the gods are unknowable in spite of human wisdom. The older 'Pessimistic Dialogue between Master and Servant' (mid-second millennium Babylonian, ANET, 437-438) also reflects (in somewhat comic vein) on the uselessness of all effort, and the common end of good and bad alike.

Ecclesiastes, therefore, takes up themes that were common in the world of its day. Orthodox Bible readers sometimes wonder how it came to be included in the canon! Its value may be analogous to that of Job and some Psalms, in the sense that it allows a certain type of religious experience, or doubting, to be honestly expressed. The canonical point can, of course, be turned on its head. The book's presence in the canon gives it a wider context within which the questions it poses may test the affirmations of orthodoxy, but also receive answers from it.

The Song of Songs

The Song of Songs is also known as the Song of Solomon, or simply as the Song. It is unique in the Old Testament, being essentially a love-song, or series of these. Like Ecclesiastes, it is associated with Solomon, perhaps because of his renowned potency in love (1 Kgs 11:1-4). Datings of the Song vary from Solomon's own time to the post-exilic period. Love-poetry is known from late second millennium Egypt, however, and there is little in the Song itself that would force a late date.

The action in the Song focuses on the love of a young woman and a young man, who speak alternately, with interventions at times from a kind of 'chorus' of the 'daughters of Jerusalem' (Song 5:9). It has certain features of a drama, particularly narrative and resolution (e.g. Song 3:1-5; 5); and the whole poem has been interpreted as a portrayal of a love-relationship from courtship to marriage and beyond. On this view, the wedding itself, and the consummation of the marriage, is at the centre (Song 3:6-5:1), flanked by tantalizing scenarios of finding and losing. Such a tight structure is possible, although it is arguable too that the Song is simply a linked group of poems with no particular centre. In any case, the view, once favoured, that Solomon himself actually features in the drama as a third character, claiming the girl at the expense of the shepherd lover, is not likely. The Solomon imagery probably serves to add lustre to the lover and the marriage (the procession in 3:6-11 is almost certainly the arrival of the bride, i.e. not the king).

The Song has posed problems for traditional religious interpretation, because of its lack of an obvious religious theme and its overt erotic language and imagery. For this reason both Jewish and Christian interpreters have resorted to allegorical readings, in which the love of the lovers is seen as a symbol of the love of God for Israel, or (in Christian tradition) that of Christ for the Church. A justification for such readings may be found in the use elsewhere in scripture of the analogy between human marriage and God's love for his people (Hos 2; Jer 2:2; Eph 5:22-33; Rev 21:2). This approach cannot, however, be considered as the primary meaning of the Song, which remains a love-poem. Even so, it plays an important part in scripture, affirming that human sexual relations have their place in God's creation. Along with Genesis 1-2 the Song pronounces this area of human experience 'good' – in contrast to religious teaching that has prevailed in certain times and places.

Daniel

The Book of Daniel stands among the prophets in Christian Bibles, finding a prominent place after the three largest prophetic books. In Christian interpretation, therefore, Daniel was primarily regarded as a prophet. This is no doubt because of the strong theme of divine revelation in the book, where Daniel is granted visions of what is to come in the future. The importance of the idea of promise and fulfilment in the Christian reading of the Old Testament no doubt played a part in Daniel's becoming one of the major prophets. The book has held a secure place in Christian piety since earliest days.

A glance at it shows, however, that it differs from other prophetic books in a number of important ways. It falls into two main sections. The first, Daniel 1-6, consists of stories set in the Babylonian exile. In them, Daniel himself and three companions, Shadrach, Meshach and Abednego, are opposed by forces hostile to God and the Jewish people, and consequently face various trials of their faith. The best known example is the story of Daniel being thrown into a den of lions because he refused to obey a decree not to pray to God, but only to the king (Dan 6). By their steadfastness and the mercy of God they survive these dangers.

The second half of the book (Dan 7-12) is composed of visions given to Daniel concerning the final salvation of God's faithful people out of persecution. These include the well known vision of the Son of Man, a figure who comes from heaven to receive the kingdom of God along with his saints (Dan 7:13-14, 27). Others feature the archangel Michael, the 'great prince' who fights in a final battle on behalf of the righteous (Dan 10:21; 12:1). Between the stories and the visions, therefore, there is a shift from a focus on the persecution of the people in a contemporary situation to a final deliverance from all tyranny. The two parts are united, however, by their affirmation of the victory of God over tyranny, and the salvation of the faithful.

This differs from the prophetic books in the sense that it does not have the urgent message to the people of God to reform their ways and so escape disaster. It is rather a word to a suffering people, that discloses to them God's plan for their future salvation. The visions in particular are a new kind of literature, which even interprets existing prophecy in unexpected ways. For example, the seventy years of exile predicted by Jeremiah are reinterpreted in Daniel as 'seventy weeks of years'.

This kind of literature is sometimes known as 'apocalyptic'. Within the Old Testament, Daniel is its only real example, although there are parts of the prophetic books which are beginning to show some of its features (such as Ezek 1; 38-39). It belongs largely to the period after the Old Testament (known variously as the 'intertestamental' and the 'post-biblical' period), and has its best examples in books like 1 Enoch, and 4 Ezra. The New Testament's Book of Revelation may also be included in the type. The main characteristics of apocalyptic writing are: angels and visions of heaven; a strong doctrine of God's control over all of history; the division of history into periods; the belief that the present world-order will be replaced in the end by the rule of God in a new way on the earth; the use of symbolism, often featuring strange animals. Most or all of these features can be found in Daniel 7-12.

Apocalyptic literature spans a period of several hundred years either side of the turn of the eras (around 200 BCE–100CE). It is sometimes explained as having arisen because of the persecution of Jews by the empires that prevailed in those times, especially Greece and Rome. The Book of Daniel certainly addresses the theme of martyrdom, which in fact became an issue in the second century BCE, under the Seleucid (Greek) rule in Palestine. For this reason the book is normally dated by scholars to the time immediately after 167 BCE, when (as we saw in our chapter on Old Testament history) the Seleucid king Antioches Epiphanes IV desecrated the Jerusalem temple. In this view, the setting of Daniel at the Babylonian court, in the Jewish exile of the sixth century BCE, is a literary device, with 'Babylon' really standing for the Greece of the writer's own day. (Babylon is also used metaphorically for Rome in the Book of Revelation.) Other scholars, however, hold to the traditional view that Daniel was actually written in the Babylonian exile.

Further Reading

Introductions to the Old Testament (these deal with introductory issues on each book):
J. A. Soggin, *Introduction to the Old Testament*, SCM, London, 1980
W. S. LaSor, D. A. Hubbard and F. W. Bush, *Old Testament Survey*, Eerdmans, Grand Rapids, 1982
R. B. Dillard and T. Longman III, *An Introduction to the Old Testament*, Zondervan, Grand Rapids, 1994
Other works on individual parts of the Old Testament:

J. Blenkinsopp, *The Pentateuch*, SCM, London, 1992

T. D. Alexander, *From Paradise to Promised Land*, Carlisle, Paternoster, 1995

R. N. Whybray, *The Making of the Pentateuch*, Sheffield, 1987

J. F. A. Sawyer, *Prophecy and the Biblical Prophets*, Oxford University Press, 1993

M. Noth, *The Deuteronomistic History*, Sheffield, JSOT, 1981

J. G. McConville, *Grace in the End: a Study in Deuteronomic Theology*, Carlisle, Paternoster, 1993

J. G. McConville, *Judgment and Promise: an Interpretation of the Book of Jeremiah*, Leicester, IVP, 1993

G. I. Davies, *Hosea*, Sheffield, JSOT, 1993

R. P. Gordon, *1 and 2 Samuel*, Sheffield, JSOT, 1984

D. J. A. Clines, *Ezra, Nehemiah, Esther*, London, Marshall, Morgan and Scott, 1984

D. J. A. Clines, *The Theme of the Pentateuch*, Sheffield, JSOT, 1979

J. Day, *The Psalms*, Sheffield, JSOT, 1990

R. R. Wilson, *Prophecy in Ancient Israel*, Philadelphia, Fortress, 1979

D. L. Petersen, *The Roles of Israel's Prophets,* Sheffield, JSOT, 1981.

E.W. Nicholson, *Preaching to the Exiles*, Oxford, Blackwell, 1970.

4

CRITICISM AND CANON

——— Old Testament Criticism ———

In the preceding chapter we outlined the contents of the Old Testament, and also began to consider the way in which the books had been composed. Our purpose in the present chapter is to think further about that process of composition, by considering some of the methods used by critical scholars. We shall then take that line of thought one step further, by considering how the Old Testament as a whole came into being, or to put it differently, how the Old Testament canon was formed.

Modern scholars, since the Enlightenment, have believed that they could identify sources which were the raw material for the books in the form in which they have come down to us. In other words, the texts as we know them were thought to have come into existence gradually, perhaps over long periods of time. The Documentary Hypothesis concerning the authorship of the Pentateuch claimed to be able to discern four documents from which the Pentateuch was formed. By it, the claim was made that scholars could discern the progress, not only in the writing of documents, but of Israel's religion itself. For the various documents were, according to the theory, not just different versions of events, but they were themselves religious and theological in character; they had their own distinctive views of God and religious matters; to an extent they even argued with each other; in short, they were the deposit of the ongoing, vibrant life of Israel.

For accuracy, it is important to notice three main strands in classical Old Testament criticism, namely Literary Criticism, Form Criticism and Redaction Criticism.

Literary Criticism

This is the fundamental type of criticism, exemplified by the Documentary Hypothesis itself. Its methodology is literary in the sense that it focuses on the formation of the literature as such. This it does by finding inconsistencies, disruptions and duplications in the text. It can operate on a large scale, as in the case of the double account of Moses producing water from the rock (Exod 17; Num 20); or on a small scale, as in the case of the flood-narrative (Gen 6-9). These examples, both of which we considered above, could fit neatly enough into the four-source theory (as J and P versions of the same thing).

Literary criticism is more far-reaching than the special theory about the composition of the Pentateuch, however. Nor is it limited to spotting double versions of narratives. Rather, it can find numerous additions and expansions to any text, with no limit on the amount of possible revision and elaboration. Literary-critical arguments often appeal both to formal features and to features that have more to do with a particular angle. A well known example comes from Deuteronomy. In Moses' preaching, he sometimes addresses his hearers in the second person singular (thou/thee, in the older English style), and sometimes in the plural (you/ye). (For English readers the point can most easily be appreciated in an older translation, such as the Authorized Version.) Thus Deuteronomy 6, which is largely singular address, switches suddenly in vv. 14-17 to the plural. For many commentators this was an inconsistency of style which showed them that different sources lay behind the present form of the text. A different kind of inconsistency has been found in Deuteronomy 7:11-12. The former verse, on this view, is thought to express a theology of grace; that is, Yahweh saves his people just because he loves them. The next verse then is thought to balance or correct this with a theology of works: Yahweh saves his people on the basis of their obedience to his laws.

For a variety of reasons, literary criticism is not the force that it once was in Old Testament studies. Modern readers are perhaps more aware than their predecessors of the dangers of imposing their own standards or expectations on the biblical writers. The result is that even a classic 'proof' of the literary critical method, such as the analysis of the flood-narrative into sources, no longer seems secure, as some modern scholars find that the supposed inner contradictions can be resolved after all (R. N. Whybray). The biblical writers, moreover, may have been well aware of what they were doing when they employed sudden changes of style, perhaps for rhetorical effect. And what are seen as different theological points of view may be put together deliberately in order to express a complicated thought (such as the close and paradoxical relationship between grace and law). This is not to say that criticism has abandoned its interest in sources. But it does mean that modern readers are more cautious about coming to conclusions about them. This caution goes with the strong modern interest in the 'final form' of the books, as we shall see in a moment.

Form Criticism

Form criticism was a successor to literary criticism. Its basic assumption is that the Old Testament contains a variety of oral forms, that is, forms of speech that were at home in a range of settings in the life of ancient Israel. This is, in a sense, a different kind of thinking from literary criticism, which assumed that the Old Testament was formed essentially by literary activity. Scholars who practised form criticism thought that they could penetrate more directly to the life of ancient Israel.

The classic case of form criticism in the Old Testament is that of the Psalms. Up to and throughout the nineteenth century, students of the Psalms had discussed their 'authorship', who had written them, and when and why. Was it David, as many of the Psalms themselves seemed to suggest? Or was the name of David simply used as a kind of convention, because of the ancient tradition of his musical ability? The goalposts in this debate were moved early in the present century, and probably irreversibly, by the German scholar Hermann Gunkel, who asked a different question.

Gunkel's concern was not who wrote the Psalms, but how they were used in the life of ancient Israel. The attractiveness of this question is immediately obvious. There is a tempting analogy to be made between modern congregational hymn singing and the Old Testament Psalms. Well-known hymns are sung repeatedly by congregations. Furthermore, there are groups of hymns that are used and reused on particular kinds of occasions: thus – to take an example from the Christian calendar – 'O Come All Ye Faithful' is sung at Christmas and not Easter. Easter has its own canon of appropriate hymns, as have harvest time and other festival occasions (remembrance services for the fallen in war, for example, when 'national' hymns tend to make an appearance). When these hymns are used, the matter of who wrote them, and still more why, is usually far from the minds of the users;

often the name of the author is not even known, let alone the circumstances, or what was going on in his or her mind at the time – although there are some probable exceptions to this, and certainly popular anecdotes (Augustus Toplady is said to have composed 'Rock of Ages' while sheltering from a downpour in a cleft of rock near Bristol).

It makes some sense to think that the Psalms might have been used and reused in a rather similar way. The 'types' of Psalms identified by Gunkel and others were noted in the discussion of the Psalms in the preceding chapter, together with possible settings.

While form criticism has a particularly clear and satisfying application in the Psalms, it could also be applied to other parts of the Old Testament. This is because of its general philosophy that our written texts have oral forms behind them that were at home in actual settings in life. Thus the laws and the wisdom sayings of the Old Testament can be studied form-critically, though not always with a clear consensus: the laws may reflect actual legal processes in Israel, or may have been more like reference books, known and consulted by academics. Wisdom sayings may have been set in family instruction, or in schools. The prophetic books too have been studied form-critically. We saw above that the prophets used certain types of 'oracle'. There are salvation oracles, for example, especially in Jeremiah 30-33 and Isaiah 40-55. It has been held that such oracles were uttered in worship settings by so-called 'cultic prophets', who were fulfilling a clearly prescribed function in doing so.

The difficulty faced by form criticism is in discerning the difference between the 'forms' that are postulated and the literary process, or work of creativity, that has brought them into the literary contexts in which they now stand. How do we know that we are face to face with a 'pure' form, or whether a prophet or poet has developed such forms creatively for literary or rhetorical purposes? The point may be illustrated by Jeremiah's 'Confessions', the name commonly given to those prayers of anguish and bewilderment which he utters (e.g. 15:15-18). The resemblance between these prayers and the Psalms of Lament has been frequently, and correctly, observed. A consistent form-critical view would be that in Jeremiah we simply have a cultic prophet who is using regular Laments known in the Jerusalem cult (and this view has had its advocates). Yet it is likely that the Confessions are actually Jeremiah's own creative use of habits of speech and turns of phrase which were known to him because he was familiar with the temple liturgies. In that case we do not have the pure forms, but imitations and reflections of them. To say this is not to deny the usefulness of form criticism. It is only to warn that our access to the life settings postulated by form criticism is probably rather indirect.

Redaction Criticism

Redaction criticism takes form criticism and literary criticism as a starting point, but is different from them in an important way. It is concerned not with 'original' fragments or units that may have existed independently before a book was brought into its final form, but rather with the process of bringing it into that form. If a book was not originally a unified piece of work, who made it into one, and what traces are left of the reasons and motives for his or her activity? Redaction criticism, then, works with the book, or other extended unit (say, the whole Pentateuch) that readers actually read.

We have met the term 'redaction' already when we looked briefly at the Book of Jeremiah, above. And it will provide a good example. Jeremiah prophesied, apparently, over a period of forty years or more. His sayings clearly address a number of different historical situations. Therefore it is clear straight away that some kind of organizing activity has had to take place in order to make of the various sayings something that resembles a book. This is evident in the fact that the so-called Book of Consolation (Jer 30-33) occupies a more or less central position in the book, highlighting the words of Jeremiah that promise salvation in the future. Similarly the Oracles Against the Nations (Jer 46-51) are placed in a climactic last place in the book, to end on a note of judgment for the tyrant Babylon – even though it had once been God's scourge of his own errant people. This is true, at least, for the Hebrew version of Jeremiah that underlies our modern translations. A quite different order was produced by those who arranged the text that underlies the Septuagint (LXX), that is, the Greek Old Testament. This shows that the work of 'redaction' was not necessarily unified or completed all at once. But the double version of Jeremiah tells us clearly that there were those whose work it was to bring order into the biblical literature, and who did so, perhaps, for definite theological purposes.

Redaction criticism may be defined as the search for such purposes. Here, the tell-tale sign is all important. In the Books of Samuel, for example, the placing of the Song of Hannah at the beginning of the story tells the alert reader at an early stage that it is going to be about the identification of a 'king', or 'anointed one', in Israel (1 Sam 2:10), and about God's faithfulness to him. In making an observation like this, redaction criticism has gone beyond the concerns of literary criticism (which might focus on authorship and date of the Song, pointing out perhaps that it is likely to have been composed at a time after the advent of kings in Israel – and therefore not in Hannah's own day); and beyond form criticism, which would show that the Song is a 'Psalm of Confidence', or perhaps a hymn, according to its original place in the worship of the temple. These things may well be so; but the redactor turns the raw material into literature by giving it a 'setting in literature' (in contrast to the form critic's 'setting in life'). This requires a broad understanding of the meaning of the whole book.

How far were these redactors actual authors? The line between the redactor as a mere compiler (a 'harmless drudge', like Dr. Johnson's lexicographer) and as an author is not easy to draw. Redactors may have had a major influence in the form of the books that we have. The 'Deuteronomist' is a case in point, that is, the writer who is held responsible for the final form of Deuteronomy–Kings. According to the classical view (Martin Noth), this work was the creation of a single author working in the exilic period who had at his disposal a mass of diverse material from Israel's past. A telling detail here might be 2 Kings 23:26, in which the author explains that judgment was decided against Judah in spite of the best efforts of its best king (namely Josiah, whose praise is sung in the main part of 2 Kings 22-23). The reason given is that there was no atoning for the mass of sin that had gone before, epitomized by Manasseh. In a similar way the author of Chronicles (the Chronicler) brings certain emphases consistently to the fore in retelling old stories. In his account of Manasseh, that notorious king's repentance is told to show how God is always ready to respond to a penitent (2 Chr 33:12-17). That is noticeably different from the Deuteronomist's portrayal of him as the most outstanding sinner in the Judean dynasty (2 Kgs 21). According to this view, redactor played a very important role in the composition of the Old Testament.

Canonical Criticism

A close cousin of redaction criticism is what is known as 'canonical criticism', the brainchild of Brevard S. Childs, and now a very influential concept in the scholarly attempt to understand how the Old Testament came into being. It has in common with redaction criticism a focus on the final form of the books that make up the Old Testament. It similarly shows a preliminary interest in the process that went on before the text arrived at its final form, but thinks that in the end this is not very interesting or important. The final form of the text is what really demands our attention and interest.

The 'canonical critic' differs from the redaction critic in an important respect, however. The former tries to unearth the motivation and thinking that led to the formation of a text as a matter of historical or literary history. There is no essential theological concern in this (although a redaction critic may in practice have such an interest). Canonical criticism is essentially theological, however, for it sees the final form of any biblical text as the product of a decision, or series of decisions, reached by and within a community of faith. The closeness of this method to redaction criticism may be seen in the fact that canonical critics sometimes speak of the 'canonical redactor', that is, the person who has made the crucial last adjustments to the text as we know it, on behalf of the confessing community. The decisive characteristic of canonical criticism, however, is its orientation to the biblical text as 'scripture', that is, as the rule of faith of a believing community.

The Criticisms and Intertextuality

These various forms of 'criticism' take us only so far in our thinking about the formation of the Old Testament. They leave us a long way short of understanding how the books came into their final form, not only individually, but as the large collection with which we are familiar. And the Old Testament is, for many of its readers, first and foremost *a* book, a work that coheres with itself, and that is held together by its all-pervasive topic, the ways of God in the world. The criticisms, by and large, do not account for the many echoes which ring from one part of the Old Testament to another, giving the impression of unity. The story of the Philistines' return of the captured Ark of the Covenant expressly recalls the exodus, and the Egyptian Pharaoh's extreme reluctance to let the Israelites (and the Ark) go out of that land (1 Sam 6, especially v. 6); and the story in Judges 19 (of a rape and murder) curiously echo the similar ones in Genesis 19. Echoes like this have led some modern writers to speak of 'intertextuality' in the Old Testament, that is, a tendency of certain texts to recall others. The Old Testament thus has a kind of unity which goes beyond the sum of its parts. How this was achieved is not within the power of criticism to recover. The answer lies partly in the nature of the subject matter, and in the reader's ability to observe similarities; it lies also, no doubt, in the creativity of the authors, and perhaps in a process of composition which was open enough to allow a certain conforming of books to each other, as they reached their final form.

——— The Old Testament Canon ———

Early Evidence

The natural conclusion of our line of thought in this chapter is to ask the question about the canon itself. In the story of the formation of the Old Testament, the various criticisms take us from the beginning into the 'middle'; the study of the canon looks at the end of it.

The Hebrew Bible, as we saw, has three divisions: the Law, Prophets and Writings. When and how did this classification of the material occur? The answer to this has to be pieced together from various fragments of evidence. A threefold division of the scriptures is mentioned by a number of writings from the early centuries of the present era, including the Jewish historian Josephus, writing in the 90s CE (*Against Apion*), the apocalyptic book IV Ezra, 14:45-46 (about the end of the first century), and the Talmudic tractate *Baba Bathra,* 14b-15a (third–fifth century). A tantalizing hint comes also in the earlier (second century BCE) Prologue to Ecclesiasticus, which refers to 'the Law and the prophets and the other writings' – does this mean that the last category was a recognized canonical division? And Jesus, in Luke 11:49-51, refers to a history of blood-letting in a phrase that looks like an A-Z of murders according to the canonical order of the Hebrew Bible ('from Abel to Zechariah', where Abel is the victim of Cain in Genesis 4, and Zechariah is presumably the son of the priest Jehoiada stoned to death at the command of King Joash, 2 Chr 24:20-21).

A number of writers dispute whether the evidence from Ecclesiasticus and Luke proves the three-fold division as early as those books, pointing to the phrase 'the Law and the Prophets' as the more typical early form, and suggesting that there was a two-fold canon before there was a three-fold one. This has been until recent times the more common view. With it has gone the belief that the final decisions were made around 90 CE in rabbinic discussions at Jamnia (Jabneh, on the coast of Palestine), where the status of particular books was decided. This would fit with the apparent fixity of the canon in Josephus, writing about that time. However, the idea of a 'Council of Jamnia' has now largely been abandoned, the Jamnia debates concerning rather the *use* of certain books (were they fit for *general* consumption?), rather than their canonical status.

In the present state of enquiry there are two points of view. Some hold that the three-fold division was in place by the time of Jesus, perhaps as early as Ecclesiasticus; others that the canon was still somewhat open, even at the time of Josephus. The larger so-called 'Alexandrian canon', found in the LXX, and including what we know as the Apocrypha, has been seen as evidence for a canon that was still open and growing in Jesus' time. It is not decisive, however, as it seems that there was no separate Jewish canon in Alexandria; rather, Christians there took over non-canonical Hebrew books along with the canonical ones. It is possible that the broader and narrower 'canons' simply co-existed, the latter being more official.

The contents of the canon are an easier matter. For Josephus, the authoritative books are twenty-two in number, while IV Ezra makes it twenty-four. These are probably different ways of reckoning the same quantity. Compared with IV Ezra's twenty-four the extra fifteen needed to make our thirty-nine are arrived at by dividing Samuel, Kings, Chronicles and Ezra–Nehemiah into two each, and the 'Book of the Twelve' into twelve Minor Prophets.

The Canonical Process

It will be seen from this brief sketch that we know very little about how exactly the canon came into being; we have only some snapshots of its existence and form around the beginning of the Christian era. It used to be thought that the three-fold division corresponded to a chronological order in which the parts came to be canonized. This can no longer be held.

There are indications, however, of the developing idea of canon. In a sense the idea is implicit in the producing of writings themselves. From early times, words that were believed to be authoritative were written down, on the assumption that they would continue to carry authority. The practice of writing down covenantal agreements goes back into Ancient Near Eastern practice, and is echoed in Old Testament covenants, especially in Deuteronomy (Deut 28:58; 31:9). Prophetic words too were committed to writing (Jer 36). In the exilic and post-exilic period we find that the people and writers of the Old Testament are aware of other writings: in the time of Jeremiah, some people can recall the words of Micah, a prophet who lived a century earlier (Jer 26:17-19); the author of Chronicles was apparently reading the Books of Samuel and Kings while writing his own work, and there is evidence of already existing literature in Zechariah 1:4; 7:7 and Daniel 9:2.

The Importance of Canon

The idea of canon has found itself at the heart of modern theological debates about the Old Testament. The subject is not merely a historical puzzle. The 'Canonical Criticism' of Brevard Childs has a strong theological motivation, and favours the view that the canon was fixed relatively early. On the other hand, critics of Childs, like James Barr, have argued against allowing the idea of canon such prominence in modern theology, on the grounds that it obstructs real theological thinking; the theologian should have the freedom to discriminate between good and bad theology, regardless of the artificial status given by the canon. Interestingly this theological viewpoint tends to favour the view that the canon remained 'open' until well into the Christian era. The study of canon, therefore, is an important part of the discussion about the nature of the authority of the Bible.

—— The Text of the Old Testament ——

Closely related to the development of the canon is that of the Old Testament text. It is one thing to discuss the authority of this or that book, but it is important to know also what *form* of a given book we mean. We saw above that books did not come into being all at once. There was a process of redaction. Furthermore, there may have been final adjustments to individual books as they were incorporated into the larger canonical picture. In any case there was the need to copy and recopy books as they circulated in different parts of the Jewish world. And we know that this activity resulted in variations in extant forms of books.

The modern reader of the Hebrew Bible is actually reading one particular text among those that have survived in the course of time. The new reader is soon aware that the text before him or her is one among many, because at the foot of each page there is what looks like footnotes. These are the 'textual apparatus', that is, a collection of information about alternative readings that are known from other texts than the one in hand. There are a great many such texts, most of them, however, dating from over a thousand years after the composition of the latest parts of the Old Testament. What are these various texts?

The Masoretic Text

The Hebrew Bible is most commonly read today in the current edition of the Württemberg Bible Society, the *Biblia Hebraica Stuttgartensis*, or BHS (at the time of writing, it is being revised). The actual text used in BHS is the so-called Codex Leningradensis (the Leningrad Codex). This is an example of the text form known as the Masoretic Text (MT). The Leningrad Codex, so-called because, along with many other extant texts, it is kept in the Public Library in Leningrad (now St. Petersburg), dates from about 1,000 CE. This may seem late for a standard text of books that may have first been written up to two millennia earlier. But that impression should be set against an appreciation of the Jewish achievement in textual transmission in the first millennium.

Manuscripts of the Hebrew Bible were preserved first in synagogues around the Jewish world. One of the most important discoveries in the history of the text was made in the nineteenth century, and consisted of a *genizah* of manuscripts in an old synagogue in Cairo. This was a deposit room for old or worn manuscripts destined to be destroyed, but in the meantime kept 'hidden'. On occasion, however, they survived, for one reason or another, and became a testimony to the extent and care of the earliest transmission of the text. Texts in the *genizah* may date from as early as the fifth century CE.

Textual transmission became in time the province of certain important schools, notably at Tiberias in Palestine and in Babylon. These were the 'Masoretic' schools, in which scribes produced manuscripts in the form in which we now know them. To the original consonantal text they added vowel pointing to help readers in the synagogues, and also a *Masora*, a kind of marginal commentary, designed to explain and thus preserve the details of the text for its future transmission. The *Masora* gave its name to the text that these scholars produced. The Masoretes' scholarly activity gave us the many texts that have survived and that are now held in libraries around the world (many of them in Oxford and Cambridge).

The most famous family of the Masoretes was the Ben Asher

family, who worked in Tiberias from the late eighth to the mid-tenth centuries. And the two most important complete texts of the Old Testament, the Leningrad Codex and the Aleppo Codex, can be traced indirectly to the last two members of this family, Moses ben Asher, and his son Aaron ben Moses ben Asher.

The Masoretes' painstaking and highly professional scholarship is in itself evidence of the reliability of the text that they preserved. But it is not the only witness. The most important discovery in the twentieth century, relating to textual criticism, is the Dead Sea Scrolls, that is, the manuscripts found in caves at Qumran on the western shores of the Dead Sea. These belonged to the library of the Essene group that we know as the 'Qumran community', who lived monastically at Qumran in the second and first centuries BCE. They included copies of Old Testament books, in whole or in part. All the books of the Old Testament, except Esther, were found there. And many of the texts are very close to the Masoretic text form. The best example of this is the Isaiah scroll, which is preserved in its entirety. The Qumran discoveries have yielded numerous textual variations, which are recorded in BHS. But in general they provide striking evidence that the Masoretic text type is ancient, and that it was carefully and accurately preserved over centuries.

The Samaritan Pentateuch

At the time of the Qumran community, however, the Masoretic text type was not the only one in circulation. Another important ancient text is the Samaritan Pentateuch. The Samaritans, as we have seen (Chapter 2), were a Jewish sect, which had its worship centre at Shechem. The breach between this group and the Jews at Jerusalem is well known from the New Testament (John 4:9; Luke 10:29-37). It is attested too in the action taken by the Hasmonaean king John Hyrcanus in the late second century BCE against the temple that the Samaritans had built on Mount Gerizim. The origins of the rift are not known, but presumably in connection with it the Samaritans had taken with them a version of the Pentateuch, which has come to be known by their name. It is only the Pentateuch that has been preserved by this group.

The Samaritan Pentateuch (SamP) is well known for its adaptation of the text to some of its own beliefs. For example, after Exodus 20:17 it inserts a command to build a sanctuary on Mt. Gerizim! However, not all differences between SamP and MT can be attributed to this biased kind of revision. SamP represents one early form of text, a type which was known at Qumran alongside the Masoretic type, though it was overwhelmed by it in the drive towards a standard text.

The Septuagint

A third major text type is known at Qumran, namely the type of text that underlies the ancient Greek translation of the Old Testament, the Septuagint (LXX). This translation was made from Hebrew for the benefit of the many Jews in the ancient world who knew Greek but not Hebrew. This was an especially important issue at Alexandria in Egypt. According to Jewish tradition, LXX was translated in the third century BCE by seventy-two scholars in seventy-two days on the island of Pharos near Alexandria (hence the name 'Septuagint', seventy). In reality, it was probably composed over a rather longer period and in diverse circumstances, though it may indeed have originated in the third century BCE in Alexandria. Its importance for the history of the text is that it was based on a different, perhaps earlier, type of Hebrew text from MT. It thus shows a number of variant readings from MT, of which the most important is its much shorter version of Jeremiah, omitting around 2,700 words found in MT, and arranging the book in a different order. SamP, incidentally, often agrees with LXX against MT. Text criticism apart, LXX has an enormous importance in Christian and Jewish history. For the early church it simply *was* the Old Testament, and some of the early controversies with the Jews are based on it.

Other texts

With the above we have identified the three main text types in circulation at the turn of the eras. There are other ancient versions of the Old Testament which bear indirect witness to the history of the text. We have already met the Aramaic Targums, translations from Hebrew into Aramaic for the benefit of the Aramaic-speaking post-exilic Jewish communities in Palestine and Babylon. The precise beginnings of written targum cannot be placed, except to say that they are pre-Christian. In addition to the Targums there was the Syriac version of the Old Testament. This apparently had its origin in the conversion of certain Syriac speakers in Mesopotamia to Judaism in the first century CE. The translation made for them seems to have elements in common with both Targums and LXX. It is not clear whether Syriac can be an independent witness to the history of the Hebrew text.

Conclusion

We have taken the story of the formation of the Old Testament from theories about the authorship and growth of the books to the evidence for the fixing of the text. There is a certain continuity between the two parts of the study in the present chapter: the attempt to establish the best text is part of the quest for the form of the book as it was finally composed. Textual criticism is therefore part of the business of interpretation, and indeed indispensable to canonical criticism and the notion of canon itself.

We have seen that both parts of the study in this chapter leave a great deal that is not known with certainty: when, how and in what form did books become canonical? Nevertheless, the picture is not one of anarchy nor such as to lead to historical scepticism. Viewed positively, it is remarkable how the text of the Old Testament has been preserved in the condition in which we have it, and that in MT we have a form of it that commands such wide respect. The work of biblical commentators has to go on, of course, and it is part of it to decide on many text-critical questions. In doing so, however, they are simply part of a larger enterprise of interpretation which has been in process since the words that we have in our Bibles were first spoken and written.

Further Reading:

On Old Testament criticism:

J. Barton,   *Reading the Old Testament*, Darton, Longman and Todd, London, 1984

C. Armerding, *The Old Testament and Criticism*, Eerdmans, Grand Rapids, 1983

N. Whybray, *The Making of the Pentateuch*, sheffield, 1987.

On the canon:

F. F. Bruce, *The Canon of Scripture*, Chapter House, London, 1988: an excellent brief introduction to the OT canon

R. T. Beckwith, *The Old Testament Canon of the New Testament Church*, SPCK, London, 1985; a major defence of the early fixing of the canon

J. Barton, *The Oracles of God,* Darton, Longman and Todd, London, 1986; argues for an 'open' canon

On canon, authority and interpretation:

B. S. Childs, *Introduction to the Old Testament as Scripture,* SCM, London, 1979, 46-106;

J. Barr, *Holy Scripture: Canon, Authority, Criticism ,* Clarendon Press, Oxford, 1983, 49-104

On Textual Criticism:

E. Würthwein, *The Text of the Old Testament,* SCM, London, 1979

E. Tov, *Textual Criticism of the Hebrew Bible*, Fortress, Minneapolis, 1992

5

CHRISTIAN AND JEWISH INTERPRETATIONS

In the last chapter we began by asking how the Old Testament was composed, and finished up by thinking about the communities who had given it its shape. That was not an accident, for the two things belong together. In the remainder of this book, we shall be concerned with ways in which the Old Testament has been, and can be, understood. First, we shall consider its use in the two religions in which it plays an important part, Judaism and Christianity. And finally (in the next chapter), we shall think about its place in the modern world.

— The Old Testament as Scripture —

If it had not been for believing, worshipping communities – principally Jewish – we would certainly not possess the Old Testament in its present form, and possibly not much of it at all. Jews preserved it in synagogues and schools, and established – as we saw – a tradition of scholarly, costly labour in doing so. Christians too spent long hours in the monasteries of Europe and elsewhere, producing elaborate illuminated manuscripts, some of which can still be seen in our great libraries. The very existence of the Old Testament is owed to vibrant traditions of belief and spirituality. As a holy book, furthermore, it is supremely important that it should be understood and followed. And in preserving it, the religions have provided, or become, frameworks of interpretation. The Christian preacher and the Jewish rabbi, as well as the Muslim mullah, all represent ways of understanding the scripture, and are focuses for its authority worked out in life. And this has been for many a matter of life and death, for as a holy book it has called people to a commitment of a sort that can require acts of extraordinary courage, and martyrdom itself.

Jewish Interpretation of the Old Testament

The period following the exile and into the first two Christian centuries brought about great changes for the Jewish people. Those who returned from Babylon were still under a succession of overlords: Persia, Greece, Rome. Many Jews never did return to the homeland, but settled in places as diverse as Persia, Egypt and other parts of the Mediterranean world. These formed what is still known as the Diaspora – the 'scattered': Judaism had not only to accommodate these new developments, but also to adjust to the rise of a great movement that began within it, but would soon stand over against it, namely Christianity.

The adjustments that Judaism faced concerned its very character. No longer a nation, it had to try to rethink itself as a people united by its allegiance to the Torah. Even the Jerusalem temple – though long rebuilt, and splendidly restored by Herod the Great – could not be a focus for Jews in the Diaspora in the same way that it might for Jews in Palestine. This need for the Jews to adjust to new circumstances was in essence a task of interpretation. The Torah was the supreme authority for all Jews; but how could it address the diverse and still changing facts of contemporary Jewish life?

There was in this period a huge amount of creative thinking about the meaning of the Torah. The outstanding achievement in this area was that of rabbinic interpretation. This has roots in the hasidic movement that found itself at odds with the later Hasmonaean kings, through the Pharisees, and in the first century BCE/CE through Rabbi Hillel. It was rabbinic Judaism that produced the Mishnah in the second century CE, perhaps the most important defining document for Judaism. It was essentially a compilation of oral laws as they existed in Judaism up to that time, thought to have equal authority with the written Mosaic law. The Mishnah then became the basis of the later and more extensive Talmud, which existed in Palestinian and Babylonian versions. The Talmud was composed of rabbinical discussions about the meaning of the Mishnah from about 200-500 CE.

The Mishnah and Talmud together exhibit two types of rabbinic interpretation, namely *halakah*, or rules to live by (the term is based on a word meaning 'walk'), and *haggadah*, which was more anecdotal and not legally binding. The Mishnah consists largely of the first. Informing all the biblical interpretation, furthermore, were seven basic principles, formulated, it was held, by Rabbi Hillel. These were intended to resolve difficulties that arose in interpretation. For example, a contradiction between two passages might be resolved by appeal to a third; an obscurity in one might be resolved by another; a principle established in one might be assumed to be true in another. An example of the last case concerns the sabbath: on the assumption that the sabbath is more holy than certain other holy days, something that is permitted on the sabbath can be assumed, by inference, to be permitted on the other days.

The Jews produced much more than the Mishnah and the Talmud in the period around the turn of the eras. The extensive literature known as the Apocrypha and Pseudepigrapha was created at this time. The Qumran scholars were collecting and writing books. The Aramaic Targums were written, and also many Midrashim, that is, expository commentaries on biblical books or individual texts.

A number of theological concerns may be identified in these writings. One is Israel itself. What was to be its destiny, and what would bring about a final fulfilment of God's ancient covenant promises for a people that was no longer independent and indeed scattered among many nations? The 'story' of Israel, as yet incomplete, underlies some of the apocalyptic writing that we have noticed. IV Ezra, for example, has visions both of a messianic kingdom on the earth and of a Paradise, and also Hell, beyond the earthly life. Its confidence about Israel's place in a final judgment is offset by some bewildered questioning of God concerning the people's present sufferings (Ezra 3:30, 32). The nature of Israel was a crucial concern at Qumran too, where the sect denied that the true Israel had anything to do with the contemporary cultic establishment at the Jerusalem temple; rather, the members of the sect were those with whom God had made his New Covenant, and he would come soon to save his true people out of the corrupt world.

Another theme is the Torah. The Book of Jubilees (probably second century BCE) illustrates this well. It retells the stories of Genesis so as to portray the main figures in Genesis as observers of the Torah. Thus Noah's sacrifice is in accordance with strict rules; Levi is a proper priest, and Abraham and the other patriarchs keep some of the festivals. These practices actually arose only later, according to the biblical account. But the author of Jubilees wanted to recast the first important figures in Israel's history as pious Jews. This is in keeping with the rethinking of sin as unfaithfulness to Torah; faithfulness to Torah, in contrast, began to be seen as the condition of the survival and ultimate salvation of the people.

Yet another theme is the nature of God's presence. A study of the Isaiah Targum, for example, suggests that the idea of God's Shekinah-presence had to be rethought in the wake of the destruction of the temple in 70 CE. Classically, the Shekinah was closely associated with the temple in Jerusalem. After 70, however, it seems that the Shekinah might be held to be present in Israel in other ways, for example at the rabbis' academic centres, or even in relation to pious individuals.

Jewish biblical interpretation, therefore, was driven by the need to understand the destiny of Israel. The effect of this on interpretation is clear at Qumran. There, the lines are drawn sharply between the 'Wicked Priest' and the sect's own 'Teacher of Righteousness'. In the 'pesher' (interpretation) of Habakkuk, the term 'the righteous' – a general designation in the prophetic book – is redefined to refer to the Teacher of Righteousness himself. In this way the Old Testament book is made to speak powerfully to the sect's immediate situation.

Christian Old Testament Interpretation

If Jewish interpretation has focused on the nature of Israel, Christians have asked instead in what sense it speaks of Christ. In the earliest days of the Church this meant, of course, a fundamental argument between Christians and Jews over interpretation. The nature of Israel, the place of the Torah, the divine presence – the main themes in Jewish interpretation as we saw – were at the heart of the encounter between the two religions. Jesus himself, as we read of him in the Gospel of John, got involved in it when he said that he fulfilled in his person the longing of Abraham to see God's promise realized (John 8:56). And the New Testament elsewhere identified him as the Servant figure of Isaiah 40-55 (Matthew 12:18-21). The second-century apologist Justin Martyr continued the New Testament's claim upon the Old when he wrote his *Dialogue with Trypho* (a learned contemporary Jew). Justin too saw the Old Testament prophecies as referring to Christ.

For Christians this battle for the Old Testament was not merely academic; they believed that Jesus was the promised Messiah, and their identity, even survival, depended on it. For this reason, the early

Church, as it worked out its creeds and confessions of faith, continued to recognize the Old Testament as its Scripture. There was more involved too than fulfilment of promise in itself. Rather, the nature of Christ was at stake. The main stream of the early Church had to assert, against some strong minority views, that Christ was truly human as well as truly divine. This was a crucial issue underlying the important creeds of Nicea (325 CE) and Chalcedon (451 CE). On two counts, therefore, the Old Testament became a vital part of the Christian mission: it contained the promises of a Messiah that Christians now believed were fulfilled in Jesus, and by the same token, it demonstrated the real humanity of Jesus, because of his physical descent from King David. Jesus' birth and infancy narratives in the Gospels of Matthew and Luke are thus closely tied in with the Old Testament story. It was because of the serious doctrinal consequences of abandoning the Old Testament (together with the infancy narratives and some other parts of the New Testament) that the second century theologian Marcion, who advocated just that, was not followed by the Church, and was declared a heretic.

It was one thing, however, to retain the Old Testament, however pressing the reasons, and quite another to work out a way of interpreting it in the Church. Saint Augustine could assert that the Old Testament taught 'nothing other than the Catholic faith'. But early Christian theologians were divided about how far it should be read according to its plain, literal meaning. Should it instead be read allegorically, according to the method used by some contemporary Jews (for example in certain Midrashim, and above all in the first century writer Philo)? Different scholarly centres favoured different approaches. The literal interpretation became associated with Antioch, where Theodore of Mopsuestia was a leading figure. The allegorical method, on the other hand, flourished in Alexandria, the home of Philo. Its leading Christian protagonist was Origen. In allegory, the Old Testament could be made to express orthodox Christian doctrine directly. For example, the story of Noah's ark (Genesis 1-9), as well as carrying its plain meaning, could also be an 'allegory' of baptism. The Song of Songs, which on a plain reading is a love song, has a history in pious interpretation as a mystical way of expressing the love of Christ for the Church.

The problem with allegory as a method is already apparent in the meaning of the word: it makes the text say something 'other' than what it appears to mean. But the attractiveness of allegory only veils a more basic question: does the Old Testament actually teach the same doctrines as the New Testament, and thus form an essential unity with it? Or does it rather tell a story which leads up to Christ, and in that case has served its purpose and become dispensable?

Christian thinking has always reflected this dilemma in one form or another. For example, interpreters of Martin Luther have often understood him to think that the Old Testament represented 'Law', while the New Testament proclaimed the 'Gospel' – though his actual position was more complex than that. On the other hand, another great reformer, John Calvin, emphasized the unity of the Bible by focusing on the concept of God's successive covenants with his people (who could be understood first as Old Testament Israel, then as the Church).

A modern echo of this debate may be observed in the different methods adopted by G. von Rad and W. Eichrodt, authors of the two greatest works of Old Testament theology in the twentieth century. Von Rad thought of the Old Testament as a story of salvation that culminates in Christ, picking up a theme in the New Testament which sees him as the fulfilment of promise (Luke 24). Eichrodt in contrast has looked more directly for theological teaching in the Old Testament, adopting a somewhat systematic approach to its material.

All these attempts have tried, in one way or another, to reconcile the need to read the Old Testament according to its plain meaning with the belief that it is Christian scripture, and therefore in some sense proclaims Christ. The rise first of humanist scholarship, then of modern critical thinking, spelled the end of allegory as a viable method of reading the text; it was not only unscientific, but too closely bound up with a kind of dogmatism that did not welcome independent thinking.

Yet careful scholarship did not mean, either necessarily or in practice, the end of a Christian reading of the Old Testament. Indeed, it has enriched the Church's understanding of its Scripture in important ways (some of which will be explored below). On the question of the Old Testament and central Christian doctrines, furthermore, another concept has been found useful since the days of the great Antiochene scholars of the fourth and fifth centuries, namely 'typology'.

Typology differs from allegory in allowing a higher profile to the plain, or original meaning, while seeing connections at a deep level between things taught in the two testaments. Thus the exodus from Egypt is both a real event in history, which says something important about absolute human power and God's concern for the oppressed, and also a foreshadowing of the deliverance of people from the power of sin. In typology there must be a common element between the 'type' and the thing 'typified'. In this case, the common element is God's desire that people should be free. As a method, typology has the advantage over allegory that it is forced to remain true to the original meaning of the text, as far as this can be known. Yet it also acknowledges that meaning cannot be confined absolutely and finally to a single proposition. Rather, if things are true – and especially if 'all truth is God's truth' – then there will be connections between them at a deep level.

Christian and Jewish Interpretation: Developments

The story just outlined shows how far the Old Testament has been interpreted within communities of belief. A friend once commented wryly to me, on my appointment to teach Old Testament at a Christian Theological College, that he thought the job should have gone to a rabbi! It seemed clear to him that the Old Testament was really a Jewish book. But this underestimates the extent to which *both* communities of belief have to 'translate' the Old Testament from a world that is distant culturally and religiously from either. If the Old Testament were 'naturally' Jewish there would scarcely have been the need for Mishnah and Talmud.

It follows that the task of 'owning' the Old Testament has been an ongoing matter within both Church and Synagogue. And the contentiousness of it is clear from a moment's reflection. Within Judaism, a range of traditions has developed. This is clearest in relation to the state of Israel. At one extreme are Zionist settlers in the West Bank (or Judea and Samaria, as they would term it – the difference in terms is a nice illustration of the interpretation point in itself) who think that the Torah (especially Numbers and Deuteronomy, together with Joshua), confers on Jews the inalienable right to possess certain tracts of land. At the other are those, mainly in the Diaspora, who dispute the claim of the *'olim* (immigrants to Israel) that every Jew should make *'aliya,* that is, immigrate - shades here of the difference between Ezra and Esther? Then again, there are certain religious Jews, even in Israel, who think the state of Israel is a false trail, and who wait instead for the Messiah to come, bringing his wholly different kind of kingdom. These different types of Judaism obviously employ quite different readings of the same biblical texts.

Christian history knows of equally sharp divisions. On one hand it has led people zealously into battle in the name of God: there was a time in South African history when the Book of Deuteronomy could be appealed to in support of *apartheid*, the godly Afrikaaners being equated with chosen Israel, while the black Africans were cast as the cursed Canaanites. English history allows for no superior feelings in this respect, for the same interpretative sleight of hand was used to justify English ascendency in Ireland. Much earlier, Christians went to spill Muslim blood in the 'Holy Land', in faithfulness to a 'Holy War' command.

These stories of contention should not lead to a counsel of despair regarding the interpretation of the Old Testament. They should lead instead to a critical awareness of the views that we and others hold, and a readiness to test our opinions by exposing them to others. There is no single key to this, but a primary requirement is a readiness to notice how far the reader's interpretations tend to support opinions that he or she already holds. There is, indeed, a critical strain within the Old Testament itself, namely the message of the prophets. There may be promises of land and well-being for a faithful people; but if so, then there must also be the voices that call for justice, care for the alien, self-criticism and repentance. Christian and Jewish interpretation alike is rightly chastened by the prophetic critique, already built into the scripture itself.

— A 'Surplus' in Interpretations of the — Old Testament as Scripture?

Aesthetic

Modern readings of the Old Testament which recognize it as scripture have tried to find ways of expressing the need to treat the Old Testament on its own terms. One Christian writer, while accepting the Old Testament as a 'Christian' book, has spoken nevertheless of a 'surplus' in it. That is, there is more in the Old Testament than is needed by Christian doctrine. There are dimensions of it that can be explored in their own right. This is partly aesthetic; there is beautiful poetry in the prophets, Psalms and elsewhere – best savoured in Hebrew for its wonderful use of sounds, yet capable of being appreciated in translation too because of its rhythmical quality. There is narrative, with all the characteristics of good story-telling: character, drama, plot, surprise, humour, appeal to the imagination. It is not for nothing that certain Old Testament stories (David and Joseph, for example) have been told and retold in forms that range from the long novel (Thomas Mann's *Joseph and His Brothers*) to the stage musical (*Joseph and his Amazing Technicolor Dreamcoat*), or that the encounter between Solomon and the Queen of Sheba has been turned into romance.

The 'surplus' is not confined to aesthetics, however. In substance too the Old Testament can be looked to in ways that are not directly mediated through later theology. One area is politics, about which the New Testament tends to speak only indirectly. The Books of Samuel, on the other hand, have much to say. The central issue there, as we saw, concerned the type of political leadership that should be exercised in Israel. Martin Buber, the Jewish philosopher and biblical interpreter, went so far as to say that these books were the Old Testament's *politeia*, that is, polity, or basis for government. The implication of this is that the debate that went on in ancient Israel still has significance for modern thinking. The modern relevance of ancient Israel's struggle against totalitarian forms of government, and its concern that systems should protect the individual, is evident. The stories also portray the conflict between the ideal and the real in political life, the potential for power to corrupt (David, Bathsheba, Uriah, 2 Sam 11); and the interplay between private and political life (David's personal and family failures have an effect on the body politic, to the great frustration of the hard-headed professionals among his personnel; 2 Sam 19:5-8). There are vivid pictures too of a corrupt society, in which all trust has gone, that have modern echoes (Jer 9:1-9). And the concern for social structures operates, finally, at the level of the family unit, with provisions, for example, for care of the elderly (see further on ethics in the next chapter).

It is the Old Testament indeed, rather than the New, that contains a theology of humanity. The creation narratives (Gen 1-3) are a reflection on humanity's position in the world, its relation to God and the relation of one to another. In them, themes of responsibility, purpose and fulfilment are taken up. Thinking about the human condition is found also in the Wisdom literature, in which patterns of civilized behaviour are explored (especially in Proverbs).

And then there is love and sex. The Song of Songs, as we have noticed, is a love song, which actually makes no reference to God. Some of its lyrics are, to use a modern phrase, of a sexually explicit nature. And the theme of this book is nothing other than human sexual love. The Song is not alone in taking up this theme, for it is present in the creation accounts too, and in a number of other boy-girl encounters in the literature: Isaac and Rebekah, Jacob and Rachel, David and Abigail (not to mention Bathsheba), Ruth and Boaz. It is true that a modern reader can spot romantic entanglements where the ancient would have been aware of other kinds of social nuance: in the norms and expectations of a patriarchal society, Boaz, for example, is a figure of moral stature rather than, necessarily, a great lover. Yet, some of our narratives take an unmistakable delight in depicting the age-old theme of erotic love.

Indeed, it is no accident that so much of the Old Testament is in narrative form, for narrative can depict the whole range of human experience. And there is nothing less than that in the Old Testament. We feel the helpless frustration of the innocent Job; the unfathomable pain of a father at the death, or imminent death, of his own son (Gen 22; 2 Sam 18:33); the grief of the woman who cannot bear children (1 Sam 1) – turned in time to joy (1 Sam 2:1-10); the dark, dangerous mood of Saul (1 Samuel 16, and caught so well in Robert Browning's *Saul*).

When we engage with the Old Testament in this way we find ourselves confronted with a book that is not only 'religious', but is the literature, philosophy and legacy of a great nation. In this respect it is somewhat like the Classics, that other great body of literature that goes to the heart of the human experience.

A Liberated Old Testament Interpretation?

In the preceding paragraphs we have noticed that, even when we read the Old Testament from the point of view of a certain religious commitment, its power to speak to modern people is not exhausted by its teaching of recognized doctrines. rather it echoes with the whole range of human experience. This facility of the Old Testament to speak to modern people in many ways has had some important consequences in modern thinking, both within and beyond religious communities. We have made the general point that meanings are not locked up within texts, waiting to be released. Rather, meanings have something to do with the situation and preconceptions of the reader. It was in this context that religious communities have tried to guard interpretation. Some modern interpretation, however, has stressed the role of the reader to the extent of claiming that it is the reader who creates the meaning of texts. This tendency has emerged most strongly in movements which have tried to read the Old Testament in terms of a special perspective. This has been conceived either as a means to revise the attitudes and teaching of religious groups, or as an endeavour quite outside the religious realm, in the broader arena of social relationships.

One powerful example is feminism. As we saw, the Old Testament has much to say, in the context of its theology of humanity, about male-female relationships. Many women writers, however, have gone much further than this observation, and have claimed that the history of biblical interpretation has been male dominated, and white and middle class into the bargain. This, they think, has skewed the reading of the Old Testament in such a way as to reflect badly on women. Men have seen the first human being as male, and the woman as the one who caused the trouble (Gen 1-3); they have read narratives as if they were 'about' men only, failing to notice that women played an enormous role in the action and issues; they have chosen their heroes (Abraham, Gideon, David) according to their bias and preferences. All this, feminist writers claim, can be turned upside down. Who said, asks Phyllis Trible, that the first human being was a man? Read Genesis 2 again, think of the first occupant of the Garden of Eden as an 'earth-creature' (the word '*adam*' resembles the word '*adamah*', 'ground', in the narrative), and the whole picture changes. A sexual differentiation comes in only at 2:22, where the 'rib-operation' is not the creation of a woman alongside the man, but the division of the 'earth-creature' into two equal and opposite beings. Not only this, but the woman in her dialogue with the serpent is not the first sinner, but the more interesting and intelligent of the two! And other feminist writers have rewritten a host of Old Testament stories recasting the men and women so as to highlight both the significance of the woman, and the blinkered nature of previous interpretation. Feminism can also reach into allied fields of study, such as biblical archaeology. Carol Meyers, for example, focuses not on the military and political high points (such as the fall of Jericho), but on the nature of ordinary village settlements, and what can be learned from them about daily life, in order to draw conclusions about the economic role and power of women.

Another example of this kind of re-reading of the Old Testament is in political theology. Once again there are solid footholds in the text for such thinking, as we have seen. And ancient Israel's 'liberation' from slavery in Egypt has become a welcome paradigm to certain groups of their own 'liberation' from oppression. The black churches in South Africa were a case in point, as are others in

Latin America. If God could hear the cry of an afflicted people then, may he not also be expected to do so in any such situation? This reinterpretation too challenges the traditional reader (or churches) to acknowledge that he or she, in spiritualizing the message, has failed to hear an important part of it, and its urgency.

There is great power in analyses of this kind. In terms of the theory of interpretation, they build effectively on the fact that texts are invested with the prejudices of their readers. They speak directly to people in particular situations, giving a sense that the Bible really means something for them. And they can expose careless, self-regarding interpretation mercilessly.

Interpretation under Control?

All interpretation, however, has to be able to criticize itself if it is to claim validity. An anarchic interpretation (which simply insists that 'this is what it means for me') is not likely to command assent. Readings that seek to revise traditional exegesis of key texts have to be tried and tested in the public domain. (Trible's re-reading of Genesis 1-3 has had both a measure of support and some severe criticism). And interpretations that make much of a certain type of passage need to ensure that they are not missing other important dimensions of the biblical message. A theology of liberation, for example, should reckon also with its counterpoint in the biblical themes of exile and suffering, both innocent and otherwise.

The elusiveness of a balanced interpretation may be illustrated by a further note on 'liberation theology'. While this typically flourishes where the people in question can identify itself (morally) with ancient Israel in its affliction, there are circumstances which complicate this. In South Africa, Afrikaaners applied the notion of Israel and the promised land to themselves before black Africans (in a neat twist) focused on their kinship with Israel in Egypt. The case is even clearer in Palestine, where Palestinians, while feeling the need of a 'liberation theology', are incapable of seeing themselves in the role of 'Israel', however defined in theory. Palestinian liberation theology, therefore, has developed as a kind of antithesis to Israeli perspectives; if Israelis appeal to the conquest traditions, Palestinians turn instead to the prophets, who taught the people of Bible times not to take for granted what they had been given. The title of Naim Ateek's book, *Justice and Only Justice*, is a quote from the Torah itself (Deut 16:20), and thus challenges with some irony the Zionist claim to determine the meaning of the Old Testament.

The last point is salutary. When we compare diverse interpretations of the Bible, we may feel that it is a hopeless task, because there is no possibility of agreement. Readings of the Old Testament, furthermore, often depend heavily on the prior commitment of the reader, or the community of belief, or the interest group. This need not be surprising. The idea of a commonly agreed, final interpretation of the Old Testament is fundamentally false. As it emerged over a long period, in the fires of a people's real experience, so its life in the modern Church, synagogue and world can also be expected to be characterized by debate, passion and growth. Its nature is not such as to settle arguments once for all, nor to allow any group to feel smug or secure. It is rather to disturb and challenge.

This, of course, is just the point that needs to be made in relation to the readings of some of the 'interest groups' that we have noticed. The problem for them is that they might only hear from the Bible what they have decided to hear beforehand; they might only 'affirm', and never put a fundamental challenge to the reader. But that is the universal issue in biblical interpretation. It is here that interpretation as an activity or technique runs up against human nature's tendency to self-assertion. It has been the Bible's fate to be allied to many causes, whether radical ones, or the maintenance of a powerful *status quo*. The Bible is a temptation, and the devil himself can quote it, as we know from his encounters with Jesus in the wilderness of Judah. This is what has to be put in the balance against the idea (true as far as it goes) that biblical interpretation is a science. To say this is not to abandon the quest for 'right' interpretations. It is only to recognize that we inevitably have a starting point in all our reading of the Bible, and that recognition is the first and crucial factor in biblical interpretation that is creative, yet responsible and self-critical.

Conclusions

The argument in the present chapter began with the general point that all texts need to be interpreted. It went on to see how the two religions in which the Old Testament has a central place have attempted to interpret it in terms of their core beliefs. In this context a methodological dilemma surfaced, namely how far the Old Testament might be read according to its 'plain sense', and how far it must be held to express doctrine. We then saw something of the wide range of modern readings to which the Old Testament has been subject, a reflection of the variety of interests with which people read it, as well as of its power to attract and influence in unsuspected ways. The different roles of the Old Testament suggest a dilemma, which will be the subject of our last main chapter: the rich variety of the Old Testament on the one hand, and on the other its claim to be 'the book of God'.

Further Reading:

Jewish interpretation:

J. Neusner, *The Judaic Encounter with Scripture*, Eerdmans, Grand Rapids, 1987
Dan Cohn-Sherbock, *The Jewish Heritage*, Blackwell, Oxford, 1988
James H. Charlesworth ed., *The Old Testament Pseudepigrapha I & II,* Doubleday, New York, 1983, 1985

Christian interpretation:

D. L. Baker, *Two Testaments, One Bible*, IVP, Leicester, 1991 (2nd ed)
J. Rogerson, C. Rowland, B. Lindars, *The Study and Use of the Bible*, Marshall, Basingstoke, 1988
J. Goldingay, *Approaches to Old Testament Interpretation*, IVP, Leicester, 1990 (2nd ed).
Ben C. Ollenburger, E. A. Martens and G. F. Hasel eds., *The Flowering of Old Testament Theology,* Eisenbrauns, Winona Lake, 1992

Literary interpretations:

T. Longman III, *Literary Approaches to Biblical Interpretation,* Zondervan, Grand Rapids, 1987
R. Alter, *The Art of Biblical Narrative,* Basic Books, New York, 1981

D. M. Gunn and Danna Nolan Fewell, *Narrative Art in the Hebrew Bible*, Oxford University Press, 1993

Political and feminist interpretations:

Christopher Rowland and Mark Corner, *Liberating Exegesis*, SPCK, London, 1990

Naim Ateek, *Justice and Only Justice: a Palestinian Theology of Liberation*, Orbis, New York, 1989

Phyllis Trible, *God and the Rhetoric of Sexuality*, Fortress, Philadelphia, 1978

Carol Meyers, *Discovering Eve: Ancient Israelite Women in Context*, Oxford University Press, 1988

6

THE BOOK OF GOD

The idea of the Old Testament as 'a book' may seem to have come into question in the preceding pages. We have seen the great diversity of its literature, and we have noticed too how differently it is read by different groups. How then can we speak of it as a unity at all, let alone claim for it the title 'the book of God'?

And yet there are good reasons for doing so. The impulse to see the writings before us as a canon shows that the Old Testament has from time immemorial been considered as greater than the sum of its parts. Its arrangement in both Christian and Hebrew forms shows that it has been received as, in the first place, a story of God's dealings with human beings. The two canonical arrangements suggest slightly different understandings of the story: Christians structure it as a progress from creation to the imminent expectation of a Messiah-saviour (Genesis-Malachi); Jews see an arc from creation to the existence of an ongoing Jewish community in the world (Genesis-Chronicles). Yet even this difference is not so great as it might appear. For Jews too have seen in their Scriptures a hope for a better world; post-biblical Jewish writings contain expectations of a Messianic sort, as well as hope of individual immortality. And Christians, on the other hand, have probably been fascinated more with the *stories* of Daniel (about saints 'in the world'), than with the *visions* in the same book, even though these make crucial links with their Messianic theology.

The diversity of the Old Testament, then, may be a kind of technical problem: how may a 'theology' be constructed out of this material? But it is not a problem at the level of the reader's encounter with it. For even in the modern world it has been received as a 'book', indeed as a book that tells about God. Yet the sense that it is 'the book of God' does not depend on this canonical point. It has become 'canonical' because it is about God in the first place. In its discourse, style and subject matter it draws us into thinking about God from the beginning. Its opening words: 'In the beginning God..', set the scene for all that follows. Individual books, as far as they fall within the main narrative frameworks, come in a sense to rounded conclusions, yet also lead on to what comes next (the opening words of Exodus and Joshua illustrate the point). And the narrative frameworks provide the broad context for the other types of literature. So it is that books that seem to speak little, or less directly, about God, prompt the question: 'how does this fit into the developing picture?' rather than the response: 'this should not be here'.

If we agree that the Old Testament is 'the book of God', however, that is only a beginning. Can we go further and spell out what it amounts to theologically? Is there *a* message of the Old Testament?

Towards an Old Testament Theology

We noticed in the last chapter that the search for an Old Testament theology had been a major concern of scholars in the twentieth century. Many looked for a concept that could be considered central to the Old Testament: was it 'covenant'; or 'Israel'; or 'communion with God'; or was it just 'God'? There was no agreement on this, and the search for a centre has been largely abandoned. One question has concerned the unity of the material on various topics. For example, do the occasional mysterious, 'anthropomorphic' appearances of God, as in his encounters with Jacob (Gen 32:24-32), hark back to an old type of religion that the more developed theology of the Old Testament has left behind? However, if we think of the Old Testament canonically, that is, as a finished whole, it is possible to outline a number of central beliefs and concerns that are bound to be part of any theology of it.

One God

First, it has a particular view of God. The Old Testament's understanding of God was expressed out of the encounter between Israel and the other nations in its environment. In its prohibition of image worship and its insistence on only one God it showed an awareness of the danger of entangling God within human processes. An 'imaged' God might be thought to be at the disposal of people, and the victim of history and circumstances. An image might be taken into captivity, and the defeat of the god proclaimed. The God of Israel withheld himself from such reasoning. In this sense he may be called 'spiritual'; that is, he is free from all contingencies; he dwells in heaven, and cannot be contained on earth in buildings made for him (1 Kgs 8:27). Whatever happened to Israel, its God was still the living God, and there could be hope of a future.

He is not only spiritual, but he is one. The central confession of Israel was: 'Hear O Israel, the LORD our God the LORD is one' (Deut 6:4). This seems to mean two things at the same time. It means that there is no other God beside him (in keeping with the First Commandment, Exod 20:3), and it means that he has inner unity, an integrity. Both these aspects of his unity are important. In being God alone, he brooks no rival power. This is extremely important for Old Testament theology. While other nations might hope to play one god off against another, this was impossible for Israel. Since God alone was God, he alone might be looked to for blessing and salvation. Yahweh could bring Israel into a land occupied by other people because he alone was God; and by the same token, he alone (not Baal) gave fertility to it (Hos 2).

The oneness of Yahweh also means his integrity. From one point of view, this can seem to be a problem. If he alone was God, then he must be responsible not only for blessing and salvation, but also for ill fortune, death and defeat. The Old Testament does not shirk this consequence. We have seen how it explained the entry of death into the world in this monotheistic universe (Gen 2-3). Furthermore, Israel's defeat at the hands of other nations was also God's doing. Israel must work out why it was that he treated them as he did. And this was the task of prophetic theology, which exposed the falseness of the people, and showed that the fault was not in God, but in them. Yet he would not be his own prisoner, and so even beyond judgment there might be fresh salvation (Deut 30; Jer 31:31-34). There is a unity in the judgment and the blessing.

The same question arose in connection with evil in general. If God was behind everything that happened, did it mean that he was the author of evil? The issue can be seen, for example, in the two texts that tell how David came to conduct a census in Israel, an act that God regarded as wrong; in the one, he is incited to this by God himself (2 Sam 24:1) and in the other by 'Satan' (1 Chr 21:1). The latter passage obviously wants to guard against the idea of God's responsibility for an evil deed. Yet the Samuel passage itself guards something important in Old Testament theology, namely that nothing can happen without

God. If that presents a philosophical problem, it is also the basis for all hope in God, as it affirms that there is no rival power in heaven or earth.

A further consequence of the integrity of God is that he is unchanging and reliable. This is the point of the context in which it comes, for Deuteronomy asserts that God is the same for all generations. He is the God of covenant, who will act for the people of the future, and require their love, just as in the case of the generation that met him at Mount Sinai (Horeb). This point about God is closely connected with the next.

God in Relationship: Creation, Blessing and Covenant

God is not only 'one', but he also seeks relationship with human beings. This is what makes Old Testament monotheism totally different from the abstract monotheism of the Egyptian Pharaoh Akh-en-Aton. God's desire for relationship is central to his revealed character. It is implied in the very act of creation. God made the world, not for himself, but as an arena for relationship between himself and human beings. The creation of the world is intended for that purpose. The climax of the first great statement about creation is the declaration that God *blessed* the human beings whom he had made (Gen 1:28). Much of the biblical story is then about this blessing. It is Yahweh, the God of Israel, who gives the rhythm of the seasons and the fruitfulness of the earth: the 'grain, the wine and the oil', to use the much repeated phrase of Deuteronomy. And this is why Israel's worship focuses on the produce of the land. In bringing their offerings they respond to the God who maintains them in life and seeks their good.

The world, therefore, exists for the people whom God has put in it; it has no life or existence in itself (we shall say more about this in a moment). And in the concept of God's blessing is the foundation for human self-understanding. In creating human beings in his 'image' (Gen 1:26), God has given them both dignity and a sense of destiny. Oddly, a belief in creation can give to humans a higher, securer place in the world than a belief in autonomy. Here is a charter for a proper human self-esteem. This is not the same as love of self, or self-obsession, but can only be realized in the context of worshipping God.

The act of creation leads into a history of relationship with people. At the beginning of the story of Israel too, God reveals himself as the one who will go with them, and this is even closely connected with the name Yahweh (Exod 3:12-15). The promised king, in time, is described as Immanuel, 'God with us' (Isa 7:14). The 'anthropomorphic' manifestations of God (for example the appearance of three 'men' to Abraham, Gen 18) can even be seen as a seeking of human relationship. And Moses is said to speak to God 'face to face, as one speaks to a friend' (Exod 33:11). Hosea and Jeremiah both imply a certain suffering of God with his people (Hos 11:8; Jer 31:20). In these glimpses of God's involvement in his world, there are hints of a kind of 'incarnation'.

God's relationship with his people takes specific forms. The most prominent idea in this connection is that of covenant. It is a covenant that he makes with Israel at Sinai (Exod 19-24) and covenant renewal becomes an important marker of the ongoing relationship between him and Israel (Josh 24; 2 Kgs 23:1-3). The covenant, in its fullest form, implies both mutual commitment and mutual obligation. It can be evoked in metaphors, especially that of marriage, as famously in Hosea (Hos 1-3). It can be broken (Exod 32:19; Jer 31:32), and great disruption of the relationship then follows. Yet the relationship goes deeper than legal forms, and God's compassion prevails over his anger, enabling a new thing to be born out of the old (Exod 34:4-6; Deut 30:6; Jer 31:31-34; Hos 11:8).

There is an important relationship between covenant and creation. In the Old Testament story, the covenant is intended as a means to realize in the end God's creation intention to bless all humanity.

God as Present: Holiness and Atonement

In the relationship with Israel, God is *present*. This can take the form of a presence in worship: God travels with the people in the wilderness, his presence symbolized by the tabernacle, in which he can be pictured as dwelling (implied in the symbolism of the tent itself), or at which he appears from time to time (Exod 33:7-11). These are two sides of a complicated picture. He does not 'dwell' in the tabernacle as if he were confined there; nor does he merely 'appear' from time to time, as if he had no permanent relationship with his people. The ideas of dwelling and coming complement each other, expressing on the one hand his faithfulness, and on the other his freedom. In any case, the tabernacle represents a meeting-point between heaven and earth, between God and people. It is a visualization of God's desire for relationship. Yet it is more than visual aid, for God is in some sense really there.

Yet God's presence cannot be taken lightly. This is one of the key points in the Exodus narrative. There, as we saw, the question was whether God could continue to go with the people that he had chosen, since they constantly rebelled against him (Exod 32-33). In the arrangements for priesthood, tabernacle and sacrifice (Exod 25-31; Leviticus) the holiness of God is represented. The people are required to recognize God's holiness by means of the rituals that surround his presence. The act of sacrifice can carry a number of meanings: thanksgiving, vow-fulfilment, adoration and atonement for sin (Lev 1-7). Often it is hard to tell which concept is uppermost. In the regulations in Leviticus, the dominant idea is atonement. This is a recognition that there is a need for purification and reconciliation between sinful people and a holy God. The supreme embodiment of these ideas is the ritual for the Day of Atonement (Lev 16). In the requirement that the High Priest, and he alone, enter the Holy of Holies once a year to make atonement for the people's sin is captured the solemnity of the covenant relationship.

A somewhat different aspect of God's presence is his *word*. It may seem odd to think that God's word is part of his presence. Yet it is a key idea in Deuteronomy (the most sophisticated theological statement in the Old Testament). Yahweh meets Israel at Horeb in his word. In the encounter with Yahweh at Horeb, Deuteronomy plays down the idea of a vision in favour of the idea of hearing God's words (Deut 4:12). The same passage shows the potency of this concept, for it allows all future generations to participate in that first encounter by means of the passing on of the words of God from one to the next. In this theology lies the seed of the Jewish idea of Torah. But the fundamental idea is simply that God speaks to his world; he may be known; he enters into an intelligible relationship with people, not simply overwhelming them with the power of his presence.

God and History: Judgment and Salvation

What has been said about God and his presence with his people is bound up with the Old Testament's understanding of history. History is an important dimension in the Old Testament. God met Israel in particular times and places, and the memory of these is central in their religious experience. This is why they keep the Passover and other feasts (Exod 12). Yet those crucial meetings with God are not locked in the past; they are not 'once and for all' in the sense that all of history is now foreknown and foreclosed.

Rather history still lies open before each generation. This is behind the idea that the experience of Horeb can be relived by succeeding generations, and behind the notion of covenant renewal. It is also connected with the idea of the freedom, or spirituality, of God. In his refusal to be 'imaged' he asserts that the nature of his relationship with people is such that it always becomes new.

This is why the Old Testament has told about God in the form of a history. It is a story that moves on. Its early stages concern God's dealings with a family (Abraham and the patriarchs); it developed with a landless people in Egypt, till they became a nation with some standing on the world stage (under David and Solomon), and finally returned to the condition of exiles, and a religious community. Yet 'finally' is the wrong word, because history still remains open, and therefore the exiles' prayer is justified and valid (Neh 9:32-37).

God's history involves judgment and salvation. We touched on these in thinking about the unity in God himself. His very character is expressed in his adherence to what is right and his abhorrence of what is wrong. This resolve to establish what is right is played out in Old Testament history. Indeed, it may be seen as the central issue in it: how may salvation be won when judgment is due? (The dilemma is expressed acutely in Hosea 11:8, as we saw.) The Old Testament's final word on this is nicely poised. It points to a victory in the end for grace and salvation. Yet it knows too that there must be a reckoning for all that has been said and done.

If judgment and salvation are the fabric of Old Testament history, this explains why so much of it is the work of prophets. If God seeks constantly to relate and to renew relationship, then Israel must always be called again to faith and faithfulness. The prophets recall the past, address the present, and point to the future. They know that they are in the midst of time, and that what is decided today is of vital significance for tomorrow. They are aware of the true nature of God, that in his freedom he may not be presumed upon; and of the true nature of humanity, that they are dignified with the capacity to relate to God, and that this brings a serious responsibility.

The belief in a 'future' should be considered a little further. The Old Testament story opens with a forward look. God created human beings in order to bless them. In time he made a promise to Abraham, and later to Israel. And that dimension of promise hangs over the Old Testament, awaiting fulfilment. Prophets, as we saw, look beyond judgment to a new age. 'In the latter days' is a favourite phrase, and they abound in images of future hope. In the 'end time' (which remains undefined) Jerusalem shall be established as the place of God's presence, and all nations shall go there to know Yahweh (Isa 2:2-4). In a bold and impossible metaphor, 'the wolf shall live with the lamb' (Isa 11:6), the vision of a wholly different world is held out. And so the Old Testament is full of the sense of movement towards fulfilment, of a realization still in the future of all that the world might be. That vision has been rounded out in a number of ways in both Jewish and Christian theology. But the vision itself is fundamental to both. Human beings know a God who has worked on their behalf in history, and he is working still.

A 'Disenchanted' World

The word 'disenchanted' is not used here in its everyday sense of 'disillusioned' – however much that kind of disenchantment may be true of a jaded modern generation. This 'disenchantment' simply means that the created world is not itself somehow 'alive'. The point may be lost on a generation that has been formed by the Enlightenment, and that is therefore used to the idea. But it has not always been so, nor has the idea of an animated world gone for ever. The Old Testament writers faced a culture that did not distinguish clearly between gods and the world. The primeval deities known to the Babylonians were at the same time the raw material of the universe. For the Egyptians, the Nile itself was a god. So too were kings, in Mesopotamia and Egypt, living embodiments of the connection between heaven and earth; the dying Pharaoh fled the earth and was assimilated to the sun-disc, like all his predecessors. The religion of the ancient world too assumed deep connections between manifestations in the world and reality in heaven. Canaanite fertility religion thought it could influence the course of the agricultural year by means of sexual rituals involving the king and religious prostitutes. Sorcerers and intermediaries of various kinds found significance, for example, in the entrails of animals, and conducted magical rituals in order to read them.

The world about the Old Testament writer, therefore, was magical and superstitious. But this was out of keeping with what he knew of God. He was not trapped in a kind of material relationship with the world: that was the point in Genesis 1, and in the prohibition of images. All that we have noticed about the nature of God, therefore, now has a knock-on effect when we consider the Old Testament's view of the world. The world in itself held no nasty surprises; it concealed no powers that could challenge or frustrate God, hence the possibility of a trusting relationship with him. God's answer to Job, who had longed for explanations, included a survey of the variety of the created world and the splendid and powerful creatures in it, only to show him that they were all *mere* creatures, subject to their creator (Job 38-41). There was no Chaos after all, for all was subject to his purpose and will – the will that was knowable to human beings through his word. If there was knowledge available to human beings it was not of the esoteric sort; it was available to them in two ways, by the natural capacities that God had given them, and by his word.

The idea of a 'living' world retains a fascination even for modern people. It has always been alive and well in eastern religions, and in the west too, many have begun to look again to 'mother earth' in their quest for religious experience and comfort. Our folk religion, with its horoscopes, is based on superstition. And there is a type of modern discourse, appealing to science, that animates nature by personalizing the forces that it thinks govern life: 'Evolution found a way..'. All this is firmly opposed by the Old Testament. The created world is merely that: Genesis (1), Deuteronomy (4:19) Job (39-41) and the Psalms (Pss 8; 104) – to name some important examples – are firm on the point. The 'Wisdom literature' in general may be mentioned here. For it is at this point that it has a profound connection with the covenantal and historical literature of the Old Testament. As that literature insists on the freedom of God from containment in the world, and the location of his activity in history, so the Wisdom literature, at least in Proverbs, assumes a created order that is predictable and orderly. The openness of the world to those who live in it is the basic assumption here – even if Wisdom can also express fundamental questions about the world that arise from human experience. And this is thus a profoundly unifying concept among the diverse literature of the Old Testament.

In the same concept lies the mandate for all human investigation of its environment, indeed the basis of modern science. There is some irony in this, considering the modern notion that science has made Genesis obsolete. In truth, the point about Genesis and science is this: that as Genesis opposed all ancient 'enchantments' of the world in its day, so it can still stand against modern 'enchantments', whether they come from the muddle of ideas known as New Age, or from the tendencies within modern science to re-animate the earth and thus abolish the need for the creator God.

Worship and Ethics, or a 'Whole' World

The Old Testament has a holistic view of the world. That is, it sees all of life as having a unity under God. It does not put religion in one box and ordinary life in another. Instead, everything is bound up together. The farmer pursues his vocation as a matter of economic necessity. Yet his work shades over into worship, because in due time he will bring the first of his flocks, his herds and his produce as an act of homage to the God who gave them. So worship flows out of the natural things of life. It is also inseparable from ethics. For the response to God is an act of the whole community, and in that sense of community lies a mutual obligation. This is the essence of Old Testament ethics (Deut 14:28-29). That topic, however, deserves separate consideration.

The Old Testament and the Modern World

Ideology

In the outline above, we finished by touching on the necessity of ethics in an Old Testament theology. If the Old Testament is 'the book of God' we might expect it to mean something for how people should live. But we saw too that in the Old Testament there is a complete fusion of religion and ethics. That is, when it thinks about how to live (ethics) it always does so in relation to God. The Ten Commandments are not, as sometimes superficially thought, just an exalted ethic, a code of behaviour that all right-thinking people should assent to. The commands are prefaced by a ringing statement about God: 'I am the LORD your God, who brought you out of the land of Egypt' (Exod 20:2). The first four of the ten (vv. 3-11) are expressly about 'religious' things – the need to worship God alone, in a fitting way. The whole code is intended to produce true worship. The same unembarrassed mixing of what we think of as 'religious' and 'moral' laws occurs throughout the law-codes (Exod 21-23, Lev 17-26; Deut 12-26), so as to make it impossible to separate out the ethical in any neat way. This is because it was entirely natural for the people of the Old Testament to think that the God whom they knew and worshipped stood behind everything that they considered right – and stood against all that they knew as wrong.

The place where this hits the modern reader hardest is in the command to Israel to occupy the land of Canaan, driving out the inhabitants (Deut 7:1-5; Joshua). This is in stark contrast to modern attitudes – the proper concern for the protection of peoples, security within accepted borders and the right of self-determination. Indeed, the Old Testament's doctrine of election can seem to disqualify it right at the start from having any modern relevance.

However, it would be wrong to take this command as some kind of paradigm for modern action. There are other things to hear in it. Fundamentally it affirms the close connection between worship and life. What is thought about God has a deep effect on how one lives, not only as individuals, but as whole societies. (One might consider in this connection a number of societies which have had a distinctive theological foundation, and think through the connection between that theology and the kind of society: the Geneva of the Reformer Calvin; modern Iran; Puritan America; Soviet Russia.) In The Old Testament, the conflict between Israel and Canaan was a confrontation between two quite different ways of understanding the world: in opposing Canaan, Israel was refusing a whole culture, and choosing another. For them it was not a choice between God and no-God; that was not an option. Rather it was a case of what kind of God. For Israel, the answer was provided by its history with the God who had saved them from Egypt and slavery; they knew what he was like, and the whole Old Testament is about what that means for the sort of people Israel ought to be. For modern societies too, it is rarely a case or 'God or no-God'. Rather, ideologies of one sort or another compete to drive society, whether the name of God is employed or not. It is in this sense that the Old Testament's radical rejection of Canaan speaks to modern society: it asks what kind of 'god' drives it, and exposes destructive ideologies. Even where states are overtly religious (Christian, Jewish or Muslim), the question remains, what is the nature of the God who is invoked here?

The Old Testament, 'Israel' and Modern Society

Before going further it is time to face a possible objection: is there any sense in which ancient Israel may relate to modern society? There seem to be arguments against the very possibility. From its basic world view to the specific issues it faced, it was so very different from most modern societies. Yet the argument can be made the other way round. In its recognition that it owed its existence to God, and in its adoption of his love and justice as the basis of its community life, it stands over against societies which seek other forms of justification. Old Testament Israel is in its constitution prophetic.

This does not mean that modern societies are called to imitate ancient Israel in every way. That is inconceivable, because there are huge cultural differences. The ethical task is to understand in what ways Israel proved faithful and unfaithful to its calling to live in covenant with God, and to see how those insights might be embodied in a modern society.

Basically, Israel challenges modern society because of its postulate of God. This is not simply a cultural difference from modern society, but a challenge to accept a biblical understanding of the human place in the world. This is only a first step, however, for there are false trails that can be followed from here. Human history is littered with enterprises that have claimed God for themselves, but which have to be judged with hindsight as having been driven by self-serving agendas. The Old Testament has a remedy against this - as we have seen in the preceding chapter – in the message of its prophets.

There is an 'ideal' Israel in the Old Testament. It consists in the people that worships God because of its salvation from slavery in Egypt; that keeps the laws he gives, enshrining the principles of love and justice that derive from his character; that is even structured according to those principles. This Israel resists in principle the temptation to allow a permanent, 'top-down' system of rule, that is, dynastic monarchy on the model of Canaan. Love and justice are embodied not only in its laws but in its worship (Deut 14:28-29).

The real Israel is somewhat different, as we know from the story told earlier in our study. Corrupt almost from its inception, it imitated the nations and flew in the face of its election. From the moment that Samuel opposed Saul's abuse of his power (1 Sam 13:13-14), or that Elijah faced down Ahab for his denial of Naboth's inheritance in God's land (1 Kgs 21) the prophets stood against this. Their genius was to recall Israel to what it was in truth, the people of God. Israel heard a message of election, and wanted to turn it into a doctrine of absolute security, and of God's intrinsic preference for them. The prophets said that election could only mean anything if it meant an embodying of God's love and justice in society, and further, if it had a vision for the extension of

God's salvation to the whole world.

It is through the prophets that modern societies might also hear God's message through Israel. Where God has been taken as an excuse to absolutize a people's own ambitions, the prophets say 'no'. It is not Israel as such that speaks from the Old Testament, but the chastened vision of those who mourned, like Jeremiah, for a covenant broken.

Having entered that important word of caution, we can go on to think of ways in which the experience of Israel, and the theology of the Old Testament, may have special relevance to modern society.

Applications

The challenge of the Old Testament to modern society should not be underestimated. It contains key concepts that cut across certain modern axioms. One such is its basic view of humanity, characterized by the 'image of God'. The idea that 'life is sacred' has a long pedigree in the history of western society, almost certainly with a debt to the Bible in this respect. But it is under severe pressure in a world in which the various branches of human studies have relativized the place of humanity in the natural order. Evolutionary anthropology has had a profound effect on the modern consciousness, for it has turned the observation that the weak go to the wall into a kind of imperative: the weak *must* go to the wall.

The most obvious consequence of this thinking is the (explicit or implicit) abolition of the concept of 'society' in the modern west. Societies are seen in some quarters as the sum of the individuals in them. The rights of the individual are supreme. And there may be a dim echo in this of the biblical doctrine of the 'image of God'. Yet a proper concern for the equality of all human beings (a gain of the Enlightenment) has been transformed in the late twentieth century into an individualism that sets people against each other in a rat race which can have only a few winners.

This is far from the biblical 'image of God', for humanity in the Old Testament is essentially social. The idea of community may fairly be seen as one of the great Jewish contributions to realizing the Old Testament's vision - although there are important echoes of its notion of 'brotherhood' in the New Testament too. There is in any case a strong social element in the ethics of the Old Testament. It was a people that God brought out of Egypt. The Ten Commandments aim at a harmonious existence *together*. The prohibitions of theft, adultery, false witness and murder, and the exhortation to care for the old, aim to achieve a prosperous life for all together. This is clear from the way in which these basic commandments are applied in the law-codes. It is there that the concept of brotherhood is developed (especially in Deuteronomy). The law of slave-release is a good example, for its understanding of slavery is not as cruel exploitation, but as a means of relieving poverty, and with the purpose of restoring the poor to full and prosperous participation in society (Deut 15:12-18). The economics of Deuteronomy everywhere provide for the abolition of poverty (14:28-29; 24:19-20). And most importantly, this fundamental idea that people belong together is grounded in an original act of God. Their identity is as 'his people', and their stake in the world is by way of an inheritance from God (Deut 4:21). The land is the Lord's (Lev 25:23); the people are his stewards.

The individual is not lost in this community. On the contrary, it is only within a community that the individual can flourish. The laws we have noticed do more than protect the poor; here is no safety net, but rather a vision for a community in which all thrive because of their fundamental commitment to each other.

These ideas have practical consequences in numerous realms. They have echoes in various contemporary political programmes, yet are different from all of them because of their transcendent dimension. The belief in a mutually supportive human society challenges elitism, together with some of the dehumanizing aspects of market economy dogma. The same concept can affect thinking in the areas of health and education, again challenging elitism. It is relevant to questions of economic aid and structural poverty, because of its implication that inequity is wrong in itself. The 'image of God' impinges also upon 'life' issues, because humanity is understood as persons in relationship with God and with each other. This is the issue underlying both the controversy about the 'beginning of life' and genetic research. Human life cannot be reduced to biological material.

The 'image of God' is not the only Old Testament concept that has modern translations. The idea of creation itself has important resonances in today's world. We have noticed that the Bible sees the world as essentially open to human investigation, being separate from both God and humanity, and given by God to human beings to 'rule'. But it goes further. The world has been given into human care for a purpose. The purpose is the blessing of human beings first and foremost. But it embraces the created order itself, as an arena within which human beings might flourish in their communion with God. This has important implications for the use of finite resources, the relationship between economic activity and the destruction of the environment, the threat posed to the world itself by weapons of mass destruction.

Undergirding all these aspects of an Old Testament view of the world is its sense of a purpose in creation. The world came into existence for various purposes. It was to be a place where people could relate together, and also know and worship God. The history between God and Israel was characterized by salvation: when the prophet said 'the people that walked in darkness have seen a great light' (Isa 9:2) he might have had in mind Israel's first deliverance from Egypt. In fact he was looking to a later event, in the Judean monarchy. But the prophecy could be a motto for the whole Old Testament vision: God was saving a people for himself. That salvation had an effect not only on the nation of Israel, or the Jews, but for all people of all times, as the prophecies in the Book of Isaiah know (Isa 40:5; 42:6). The Old Testament teaches, therefore, that the world has a future. It is a future that is in the gift of God. But human beings are called into his service as they move into that future with him. And this basic concept affects every human thought and action. For everything is brought under the judgment of God's purpose for his world.

An Ecumenical Imperative?

We have spoken hitherto in the present chapter of a 'book of God'. As for who that God is, we have let the Old Testament speak for itself, as it were. Yet we know from the preceding chapter that 'God' has come to mean different things for different people. In particular, the three religions that share the Old Testament have developed their very distinctive ways of thinking about God. Might the Old Testament, nevertheless, be a ground on which the religions might meet? Rabbi Jonathan Sacks and others have spoken of 'an interfaith imperative' in a world which is by many measures 'post-religious', although by others the religions continue to have both influence and responsibility. Specifically, some have seen the Old Testament precisely as an ecumenical opportunity.

At first sight there are hopeful signs. Abraham is a key figure to all three. Did he not walk peaceably through ancient Canaan, calling his God by the name of 'El', the name of the Canaanite High God (El

Shaddai: God Almighty; El Elyon, God Most High)? This ecumenical spirit has modern echoes. The Christian visitor to the Tombs of the Patriarchs in Hebron may be surprised to find that the building housing the tombs is both a mosque and a synagogue. He or she might also be taken aback to find that the enthusiastic Muslim guide speaks reverently about 'the father' when referring to Abraham. The Abraham of the Christian Old Testament has a life in spiritualities well beyond the Christian pulpit and Sunday School. Surely there is scope here for a meeting of minds and hearts.

Yet the same Hebron has a grim place in the annals of recent relationships between the religions, for it was there in February 1994 that a fanatical Jewish settler massacred Muslims at prayer in the mosque. The act prompted revulsion from other Jews. The Chief Rabbi (in Britain) wrote at the time:

'Violence is evil. Violence committed in the name of God is doubly evil. Violence against those engaged in worshipping God is unspeakably evil. In the name of God I pray that in the light of today's tragedy no effort is spared to ensure the safety and security of the three great world faiths to express themselves freely in the Holy Land.'

(Jonathan Sacks, reproduced in *Faith in the Future*, p99)

This statement sums up the terrible dilemma in the relating of the three faiths. The act of violence (not the first in the history of the three faiths) expresses in an extreme way their birth in contention with each other. The reaction of the rabbi, on the other hand, vents the frustration of those who feel instinctively that the common heritage should lead to fellowship, not hatred.

It is at this point that the idea of 'the book of God' has its most urgent expression in the modern world, and is at the same time most severely tested. If this is indeed the book of God, might there not then be peace? The instinct that asks this has sought to show that the three ways are more one than three. If there is to be hope for the modern world, says Hans Küng, the religions must give common voice to their shared ethical inheritance. Let differences be made secondary, for the sake of the common good.

This is a noble aim. Yet it may not take seriously enough the real divisions between peoples. An alternative is to stress the responsibility of each of the faiths to explore and teach the resources within it for peace and justice. Too often contention arises between the faiths and their people because they have not understood the full range of their own traditions. We recall that the specifically religious danger is to use a form of religion to promote a cause. The best ecumenical hope has two sides. The first is a sensitive rediscovery of the resources that lie within one's own tradition. The second follows, namely the security to dialogue with people of other faiths on matters that do not threaten by definition the integrity of any. In such a programme, the Old Testament, understood through its own prophetic lens, can play a unique role.

Further Reading

G. Josipovici, *The Book of God*, Yale University Press, 1988

K.-J. Kuschel, *Abraham: a Symbol of Hope for Jews, Christians and Muslims*, SCM, London, 1995

K. Cragg, *To Meet and to Greet,* Epworth Press, London, 1992

J. Sacks, *Faith in the Future*, Darton, Longman and Todd, London, 1995

O. O'Donovan, *Begotten or Made?* Clarendon Press, Oxford, 1984

C. J. H. Wright, *Walking in the Ways of the Lord*, Apollos, Leicester, 1995

R. T. Beckwith and M. J. Selman eds., *Sacrifice in the Bible*, Paternoster, Carlisle, 1995

INDEX

creation 26, 29, 31, 65, 69, 79, 99, 111, 142, 148, 150-151, 154-155
Crete 8
Cyrus 59
Cyrus Cylinder 59

Dagon 16
Damascus 10, 54
Daniel62, 87, 108, 114-115, 147
David 2, 9, 13-14, 19, 39, 44, 46-49, 50-51, 59, 61, 80, 83-85, 87, 91, 96, 101, 105, 108, 119, 137, 140-142, 149, 153
Dead Sea 10, 11-14, 63
Dead Sea Scrolls 63, 128
Decalogue (see Ten Commandments)
Deuteronomic History 82
divine warrior (Yahweh as) 70-71, 76
Documentary Hypothesis 80-81, 117-118

Ea 26
Ecclesiasticus (Sirach) 61
Ebal, Mt. 82
Ecclesiastes 111-112
Edom, Edomites 8, 31, 77
Egypt, Egyptians 5-9, 10-11, 15, 24, 28-32, 35, 40-42, 44, 50-51, 53-56, 71-73, 75, 78, 91, 93, 109, 123, 129, 133, 137, 142, 150, 153-154, 159, 161
Eilat (Elath) 10, 12
El 27-28, 38-40, 49, 70, 78, 161
el-Amarna 16, 30, 38, 44
elders 21-22
election, choice 69, 74, 156, 158
Ellil 25
Esau 69

Essenes 62, 128
Esther 63, 104, 128, 138
ethics 140, 156-161
Euphrates 5, 9
evil 149-150
exile, the Babylonian 57-60, 80, 82, 86-87, 89, 97, 101-102, 106-107, 114-115, 122, 143, 153
exodus, the 10, 40-41, 43, 70, 73, 75, 97, 99, 137
Ezekiel 99
Ezra 59-60, 103-104, 138

family 17-18, 20-21, 35, 65, 140
farming 13, 16, 108, 154
father's house 18
feminist, feminism 24, 142
fertile crescent 5, 38
flood-narrative(s) 69, 80, 118
form-criticism 105-106, 119-121

Galilee (Sea of) 10, 12-13, 15
Gerizim, Mt. 61, 82, 128
Golden Calf 42, 73-75, 77
Greek, Greece 7, 9, 63, 65, 115, 129, 133

Hadad 27
Hammurapi 27
Hannukah, Feast of 62
Hapiru 43
harvest 72
Hasidim 64-65, 133
Hasmonean(s) 62, 128, 133
Hellenism 61-63
Heller, Joseph 2
Herod the Great 62
Hexateuch 82
High Priest 74
history 34, 41, 64, 81, 83, 86, 94, 96, 99, 115, 150, 155

Hittites 8, 38
holiness 74-75, 78, 81, 98, 151
Horeb (see Sinai)
Hosea 56-57, 95, 98-101, 151, 153

Idumeans 63
images 42, 52
Indus 9
Isaac 141
Isaiah 56, 88, 90, 93, 100, 161
Islam 1-2
Ishtar 27
Israel (modern)   140

Jacob 2, 35, 39, 69, 141, 148
Jeremiah   20, 22, 55, 88, 93-
94, 95-96, 98, 101, 120, 121, 125,
151, 159
Jericho 12-13, 17, 43-45, 82, 142
Jeroboam   51-53, 89, 91
Jerusalem   8-9, 13, 15, 38, 45,
47-55, 59, 83-86, 88, 91, 93, 96,
100, 105-107, 111, 115, 120, 128,
133-134, 153
Jesus Christ 1, 113, 125, 136-
137, 144
Jews, Jewish 2-3, 60-63, 65, 89,
102, 108, 113-115, 124, 125-126,
132-133, 138-140, 157, 159, 161-
163; Jewish interpretation, 133-
135, 138-139, 144, 147, 154
Jewish revolt 63
Job   109-111, 141, 155
Jonah 104
Joppa 10
Joseph 2, 10, 19, 35, 40, 69, 108,
140
Josephus 124-125
Joshua 13, 15, 43-45, 47, 76, 81
Josiah 54-59, 79, 86, 101, 122
Josiah's Reform   55, 80, 86

Jubilee 19
Judaism 1, 62-63, 103, 112, 129,
133, 138
judges 21-23, 23, 35, 45-47, 83,
104

Khufu 7, 30
king, kingship 15, 18, 19, 25-27,
29-31, 45-50, 50-51, 54-58, 71-72,
82-87, 96, 101, 105, 115, 122, 151,
154, 161
King's Highway 10
kinship 17-19

Lachish 53
Lamentations 107-108
law, law-codes 19-23, 71-74, 77,
91, 94, 96, 103, 120, 156, 158,
160; oral laws, 133
levirate marriage 20-21
Levites 76
liberation theology 142-143 (and
see political theology)
literary criticism 118-119

Maccabeans, Maccabean revolt
61-62
Malachi 60, 89
Marcion 136
Marduk (Bel) 26, 26, 59, 97, 109
marriage   22-23, 27, 69, 98,
104, 113, 151
mathematics 7
Megiddo 10, 13, 91
Merenptah 44
Mediterranean 5, 10-12, 133
Melchizedek 39, 49-51
Mesopotamia 5-9, 11, 24, 25-26,
29-32, 38-39, 50, 57, 71, 154
Messiah   47, 59, 96-97, 101,
103, 135, 138, 147
Michelangelo 2

Middle Kingdom   7
Midian, Midianites 14
Midrash 103, 134, 136
Milcom 31
Mishnah 2, 103, 133-134, 138
Moab, Moabites   8, 9, 10, 31,
52, 71, 76-77, 104
Molech 25
monarchy (see king, kingship)
monotheism 30-31
Moses 1-2, 11, 41, 60, 65, 70, 73-
74, 79-81, 118, 151
Muhammad 1
Muslim(s) 2, 133, 137, 157, 162
myth 27, 53

Nehemiah   59-60
New Covenant 95, 96, 99, 134
New Kingdom 7
New Testament 1, 13, 62, 115,
128, 135-137, 140, 159
Nile 7, 9, 28, 154
nomads 14
Noah 68, 134, 136

Old Kingdom 7
Osiris 29-30

Palestine 7-13, 15, 27, 38, 47, 49,
55, 63, 115, 124, 127, 129, 133,
143
Passover 41, 70-72, 74, 152
Pentateuch 65-81,128;
authorship of, 76-77, 117-118,
121
Pentecost 72
Persia 7, 9, 61, 63, 103, 133
Pharisees 63, 133
Philistines 8, 10, 13-14, 84, 123
Philo 136
Phoenicia 10, 16, 25, 89

poetry 14, 92-93, 110, 113, 139
politics 15-17, 26-31, 38, 45, 52-
54, 58, 61, 71-72, 84, 90-91, 142-
146, 160
presence (of God) 73, 151
priests 22, 32, 38-39, 46, 49, 61-
62, 73, 76, 80, 152
priestesses 25, 27
primeval history   69
prophets 10, 22-23, 58-59, 87-
102, 120, 126, 139, 153, 158-159
Proverbs 108-109
Pseudepigrapha   134
Pyramid Age 7, 30

Queen of Sheba 11
Qumran 65, 128-129, 134-135
Qur'an 1-2, 40

rabbis, rabbinic interpretation
133-135, 138
Rameses II 41
Ras-Shamra 16
Re' 29, 40, 48
redaction criticism 121-122
redemption, Redeemer   20-21
Rehoboam   51
repentance 94-95, 99-100, 122,
139
Revelation, Book of 115
ritual prostitution   25
Rome, Romans 8, 9, 31, 63-64,
115, 133
Ruth 21, 104, 141

sabbath 77, 134
sacrifice 25, 32, 38, 72, 74, 79,
81-82, 134, 152; of children 25
Sadducees   62
Samaritans 61, 128
Samuel 46, 87, 158